Getting to Know
Jesus *(Again)*

T0268990

Getting to Know Jesus *(Again)*

Meditations for Lent

Peter M. Wallace

Church Publishing
NEW YORK

Unless otherwise noted, the Scripture quotations contained herein are from the New Revised Standard Version Bible, copyright © 1989 by the Division of Christian Education of the National Council of Churches of Christ in the U.S.A. Used by permission. All rights reserved.

Portions of this book are adapted and revised from Peter M. Wallace, *The TruthQuest Devotional Journal* (Nashville: B&H Books, 2000).

Church Publishing
19 East 34th Street
New York, NY 10016

www.churchpublishing.org

Cover design by Jennifer Kopec, 2Pug Design
Typeset by Denise Hoff

Library of Congress Cataloging-in-Publication Data

Names: Wallace, Peter M., author.
Title: Getting to know Jesus (again): meditations for Lent /
    Peter Marsden Wallace.
Description: New York : Church Publishing, 2017. | Includes index.
Identifiers: LCCN 2017020494 (print) | LCCN 2017035110 (ebook) |
    ISBN 9780819233622 (ebook) | ISBN 9780819233615 (pbk.)
Subjects: LCSH: Lent--Prayers and devotions. | Jesus Christ--Person
    and offices--Prayers and devotions.
Classification: LCC BV85 (ebook) | LCC BV85 .W3175 2017 (print) |
    DDC 242/.34--dc23
LC record available at https://lccn.loc.gov/2017020494

Printed in the United States of America

For Tyler and Haley

Contents

Introduction

What It's All About

Jesus said, "I came that they may have life, and have it abundantly" (John 10:10). That's the kind of life everybody wants: full, rich, enjoyable, fulfilling, meaningful, overflowing. A lively life. The kind of life you can't wait to wake up for in the morning. A life of learning and giving and sharing and growing.

That's the kind of life Jesus wants you to have. But experiencing it comes from spending meaningful time with him. Reading his words and works in the gospels. Praying. Listening to him. Talking to him. Trusting him.

That's what this book of meditations for Lent is designed to help you do: to get to know Jesus better. Perhaps for the first time, or maybe to refresh your relationship with him. And, as a result, to make life a more abundant and authentic experience for you. One that will last forever.

Lent is a journey of the mind, heart, and spirit from the ashes of humanity to the cross and beyond—to the empty tomb. The central figure accompanying you in this journey is Jesus.

But who was he really? Why did he come and minister among us? How can his teachings transform and empower our lives? Why did he die? What does his resurrection really mean? These are questions that spur believers of all ages to seek a deeper understanding and appreciation of the Son of Man in their lives.

Between these covers are fifty-two chunks of Scripture for you to read day by day during Lent (or anytime). Just about all of them are words directly from Jesus's mouth as recorded in the Bible. They were first spoken to people pretty much like you and me a little over two thousand years ago. And they can be just as powerful today.

As you read and meditate on these verses and the devotional thoughts, you'll move through the life and ministry, the words and works of Jesus, with the goal of getting to know him in fresh ways that encourage a stronger faith and a spirited engagement with the world around you. Starting on Ash Wednesday and moving through Easter and the week after, you'll get to know Jesus (again) in a way that will move you to love and serve him more meaningfully. That's what living an abundant life is all about.

Listen to Jesus. Think it all through. I'll offer some questions to help focus your thoughts, meditate on what he means, and work it out in your own day-to-day life, and you'll need a Bible for some of them. Use the questions as springboards for your own thinking or journaling, or as discussion starters in small groups.

To get the most out of this book, either individually or in a group, you have to work with it. It's not just something to pick up each day and read and put down. I hope you will wrestle with it. Write. Think. Pray. Make what you learn about and from Jesus part of your life.

It's amazing what can happen if you do that. Jesus becomes more real to you. Life's pains and fears may seem to pale. The future seems more friendly and hopeful. Your life purpose starts coming into focus because you trust Jesus more and more. You just may start to live an abundant life.

Not that the hassles and pains and even tragedies of life will go away. But you've got someone to share them with, to go through them with. Someone to help you figure out where you're going and why. Someone to challenge you to grow. Someone who is closer to you than a best friend, a brother or sister. Someone named Jesus.

Ready?

Use these guides to get the most out of your reading each day.

» Get Real This section asks some pointed questions to help you figure out what Jesus's words have to do with you and your life.

» Dig In Here's some help to go deeper into the meditation's Scripture reading, pointing out some things you may have missed or might want to study further.

» Read On This takes you to some other part of Scripture to add to your understanding of what Jesus says or to show you what happens when you really believe what he's saying.

» Take Off A springboard to prayer—talking honestly with God— in light of what you've read and thought about, with some ideas on what your next step might be.

Spending Time in the Quiet

When are you ever quiet?

When does life slow down long enough that you can take a few minutes to look at the big picture, get in touch with God, meditate and pray, learn more about your life and its meaning and purpose?

That's the problem. Life doesn't slow down. Unless you make it slow down. And you really need some time in the quiet each day to make any sense of the noise of the rest of your life.

Even just ten or fifteen minutes a day can make a huge difference in your attitude. But it has to be ten or fifteen minutes well spent. Not cursory. Not catching a quick nap. Not getting stuck in your head mulling over your problems, but really spending time in the quiet with God.

Here are some things to keep in mind as you get started:

Make it happen.
You need to set aside the time intentionally, carve it out of your packed

schedule and stick with it. Maybe you're a morning person—so get up fifteen minutes earlier (it won't kill you, honest). Maybe you're a night person—so spend the last fifteen minutes of consciousness with God. Maybe you're neither—so catch some moments on your lunch break or right after work. There really is a fifteen-or-so-minute chunk of time in your schedule you can use. Figure out when it is for you and grab hold of it.

Get into the habit.

Commit yourself to having a time for quiet meditation every day for just one week. See how it affects your day. Then commit to continuing with the practice through Lent. By then you'll probably have developed a lifelong habit—one that's actually good for you.

Keep your focus on God.

If you only have a few minutes to spare, reading a portion of Scripture is the best thing you can do. Of course, in this book you'll find a brief scripture text each day. You can also use the Daily Office lectionary, or try Morning or Evening Prayer in your Book of Common Prayer, or online, or through an app. God's word can open your eyes to purpose, meaning, and joy in your life. It can help you handle life's tough times in authentic ways and guide you into a more meaningful future.

Pray.

Take some time to talk with God honestly and openly. Not just in your meditative time, but anytime. Anywhere. Jesus is always with you, so why not talk with him about whatever is on your mind or facing you in your day?

Use a devotional guide, but don't stop there.

Here's a good place to start: the book you hold in your hands. But beyond Lent, keep going. There are lots of great books and resources to guide your meditation time, such as *Forward Day by Day* or other devotional books from Church Publishing. They provide scriptures to read, insights to understand and wrestle with personally, perhaps some prayers and other resources to make your time as valuable and enjoyable as possible. But be sure to leave time for your own thoughts and prayers, your own conversation with God.

Capture your thoughts in a journal.
Using the questions in this book will help you develop a practice of recording your own thoughts and insights. Once you've finished this book, keep going with your own journal to record "aha" moments you find in the Bible, your prayers and how they're answered, life events and how God was part of them, and so on.

Enjoy it!
A meditation time is not supposed to be punishment, hassle, or drudgery. Think about it: It's a concentrated time when you and the compassionate God of the universe can get together and experience each other's company. It can change your attitude about everything going on in your life: the difficult challenges, the questions and fears and doubts you're wrestling with. Try it. Look at your time in the quiet as a window of opportunity you can throw open to let a little heaven into your life day after day.

Who Is Jesus?
Everybody assumes they know what kind of a person Jesus was. After all, he's been portrayed in countless movies and miniseries, in paintings and songs and books. Yet we still struggle with understanding who he really was and is.

What was he actually like? What kind of personality did he have? Was he delightful to be around . . . or demanding? Or both?

In a sense, the Bible talks about Christ from beginning to end. Before he came to walk this earth, we catch glimpses of him in the Hebrew Scriptures, in the promises of God, in the prophetic books, even in the

Psalms. And after his resurrection the rest of the New Testament helps to fill in our understanding of the faith.

In between, through the four Gospels—Matthew, Mark, Luke, and John—we get the best picture of Jesus. His personality and emotions. The way he talked to people. His honesty and directness. His love and care. His sense of humor. His easy, authentic manner. His ministry among hurting people, touching and healing and weeping and challenging and even raising them from the dead.

We often use titles today to help identify ourselves. In the work world you may have a business card with your name and a title—"manager," "sales associate," "president," "flunky," "head of lettuce." The Bible gives Jesus dozens of titles. Let's consider four of them to see if we can get a grasp of some of the most important aspects of his identity.

Four Snapshots of Jesus

The Bible reveals that Jesus was fully human and fully divine. He was God from the very beginning, from the infinite past, with all the authority and power of God. He was also a human being—born of a woman, raised through childhood into adulthood. He experienced life just like we do, with all the pain and sorrows and temptations. And with all the emotions of human life. As the God-Man, Jesus served humanity in four main capacities:

1. **Savior** (see Rom. 1:3–4). He came to earth to save us from our own worst selves. His death showed us how serious this is, demonstrating his love for us all in the ultimate sacrifice of his life. And his resurrection put an exclamation mark on that eternal statement of love. As a human being, he is able to represent us, giving his death a pure purpose. As God, he is able to be with us now and always.

2. **High Priest** (see Heb. 4:14–16). As a priest, Jesus was charged by God to be the intermediary between God and God's people. As a human being, Jesus was able to show people what God is all about in the flesh. As God, he serves as an Advocate, representing believers before God, clothing us with his righteousness and identity.

3. **Judge** (see John 5:22). Only God can really judge the actions and motives of people. Jesus came as a human being to guide us into what's righteous, holy, and good in life. He knows what's inside our hearts, so as God he judges righteously. But Jesus tells us it is God's job to judge others, not ours.

4. **Guide** (see 1 John 2:6). We're encouraged to walk as Jesus walked, to live in a way that keeps God's purpose for us always top of mind. As a human, Jesus served as our example for righteous living. As God, he is able to give us the power, strength, and wisdom we need to live as God calls us to live.

Here's something to keep in mind: reading the Scriptures will help you understand Jesus better, and understanding Jesus better means you can live life more fully and joyfully. But don't get stuck with the idea that Jesus was only around two thousand years ago. He's still here. He's with you. He's within you. He's there for you, no matter what you have to face in life.

Let the meditations in this book introduce you more fully to the real Jesus. And let them spur you to spend time with him in the spirit. It may take a lifetime, but you will slowly, surely begin to know within your very soul who Jesus is. And who you are.

What do Jesus's names and titles mean?

» *Jesus:* His name is similar to the Hebrew name "Joshua," which means "the Lord saves" (see Matt. 1:21).

» *Christ:* No, it's not his last name. It's a Jewish title meaning "the Anointed One." The One chosen by God to love and serve humanity. *Christ* comes from a Greek word used to translate the Hebrew word we know as *messiah* (see Luke 9:20).

» *Lord:* This means he's the sovereign of all, operating under the authority of God the Holy Parent (see Acts 2:36; 1 Cor. 15:24–28).

» *Immanuel:* This name means Jesus is "God with us" (see Matt. 1:23). And God really is, whether we realize it or not.

» *Son of God:* This title refers to his ultimate divinity, revealing his equality with God (Mark 1:1).

» *Son of Man:* One of Jesus's favorite names for himself (see Mark 2:28), this title acknowledges his humanness as well as likening him to the glorious one the prophet Daniel foresaw (Dan. 7:13–14). It points to what God wants for each of us—being utterly, fully, authentically human as God created us to be.

Think About It
Getting Ready for Lent

Read Isaiah 58:1–12; Matthew 6:1–21

As a newly ordained priest a few years ago, it took me some time to get used to wearing a clerical collar.

I'm still a little surprised at the double takes it can cause. For instance, I go into a local pharmacy a couple of times a month. When I walk in as a civilian, none of the people working there seem to pay any attention. But twice I've walked in wearing my collar and both times a cashier hollered a hearty "Good afternoon" to me. Maybe they want a blessing.

Not long ago I needed some plumbing work done at my condo. I stayed home that morning and waited for the plumber and his assistants to come replace my water heater and do some other projects. When the three arrived I was just wearing a sweatshirt and jeans. But I had a church-related function to go to. So while the plumbers were working I went into my bedroom, closed the door, changed my clothes, put on my collar, and then opened the door and came out. You should have seen the double takes those three plumbers made in unison (I'm not sure if that helped or hurt me when they wrote up the bill).

So I'm still getting used to the funny glances, sometimes the smiles and warm greetings, other times a frown or a suspicious look or just an expression of surprise, when I wear my clerical collar.

Well, Ash Wednesday is a day you can experience the same sort of double-take phenomenon. Maybe after the service you attend you'll go out to eat or stop at a supermarket to pick up a few things with the ashen cross still smudged on your forehead. Pay attention to the looks you get. Perhaps a conversation will arise with your cashier or server or someone you pass by who asks you about the smudge on your forehead. I've noticed people can be so helpful on Ash Wednesday—"Oh, hey, you've got a little dirt on your face. . ."

Take notice of any reactions you get. And think about why you're doing what you're doing. Who knows, it might open an interesting and life-giving conversation with someone.

But is that why we participate in this strange liturgical rite as we begin the season of Lent—just to get noticed? Why do we walk around with a cross-shaped ashen smudge on our foreheads for the rest of the day, until we wash our faces for bed?

And what about the gospel text where Jesus seems to be telling us not to show off our piety (Matt. 6:1-18)? For instance, he says if we're fasting we should clean ourselves up and look normal, not draw attention to ourselves and our great devotion by wearing sackcloth and ashes. Jesus says only God should know what we're up to.

Of course, some of us might consider Jesus's words here an easy out—we can clean off the smudge right after the Ash Wednesday service so we don't have to engage in an awkward conversation about what's on our forehead and why.

But this teaching of Jesus is a little confusing because elsewhere in the gospels, in Matthew 5 for instance, he encourages us to let our light shine so others may see our good works and give glory to God. So why is he all about being secret in this chapter—right when we get to carry this mark of ashes on our forehead?

Well, we aren't doing it to impress God, who already knows what's in our hearts, even the secrets. In fact, if we're proud about our smudged forehead then we're doing it wrong. After all, in Isaiah 58:1–12, God says, I don't want you moping around in sackcloth and ashes. No empty rituals, please. Instead I want you to get to work for the kingdom. Help somebody. Serve the needy. Give. That's righteousness in action.

And Jesus echoes this. He wants to see us at work for God's

commonwealth as well—practicing our faith, giving our resources to care for other, praying, letting go of our own wants. Putting our spiritual lives into action—positively, helpfully—is a vital, lifegiving way to demonstrate our piety and our faith to the world around us.

So maybe we get the ashes on our foreheads not as a mere ritual, trying to prove something to God, and not to impress others about how good we are in order to get a righteous pat on the back, but rather we get them for our own selves. We can't see the ashes unless we look in a mirror, and Lent is a good time to look in a spiritual mirror. To look deeply, prayerfully, into our souls and see what's lacking, what we yearn for, what we need to get back on track. The ashes remind us of our need for humility.

But we need to be clear about what humility really is. It's not some perverse opposite of pride where we whine, "I'm nothing, I'm a nobody." No, real humility is understanding and accepting ourselves as human beings in the great scheme of things, yielding our stubborn will and selfish desires to God. Humility is about knowing and accepting, even reveling in, who we are—human beings who need God wholly, and with whom God loves wholly.[1]

The ashes are for each one of us. To remind us of humility, and also to remind us of mortality. Remember that you are dust, and to dust you shall return. We hear those words as we receive the ashes. They remind us that we are mortal human beings—each one of us will die.

A few years ago around this time, theologian and Episcopalian Marcus Borg wrote this about Ash Wednesday: "None of us knows when we will die. Could even happen later today. Or tomorrow. Or maybe not for many years. We don't know. Thus it is wise, prudent, and

---

1   For some of the ideas in this essay I am grateful to the Rev. Dr. Amy Richter, "What Audience? Ash Wednesday," *Sermons That Work*, March 5, 2014, http://episcopaldigitalnetwork.com/stw/2014/02/18/ash-wednesday-abc-2014/.

necessary to repent" in order to be in a right relationship with God.[2] Marcus died within a year of writing that.

So the ashes of Ash Wednesday are also a reminder of our mortality. Borg noted that a friend of his believes Ash Wednesday is "the most honest service of the church year."[3]

Let the ashes remind you "that you are dust, and to dust you shall return." Yes, you can hear echoes of the creation story in Genesis, when God made human beings from the mud, dirt, and dust of the ground. We may be dust, but we are beloved dust. And God can do amazing things with plain dirt once it's filled with the very breath and Spirit of God.

So this Lent, let us look deeply into that spiritual mirror and see the ashes every day, not just on Ash Wednesday.

This Lent, let us continue to learn to trust that God is good and gracious and loving and forgiving, and that what other humans think of us isn't anywhere near as important as our relationship with God—and what we do for others out of that relationship.

This Lent, let us take up a discipline of doing something positive solely for the purpose of pleasing God, or perhaps giving something up in order to make room in our lives for God's Spirit to move around more freely in us.

This Lent, let us make God the focus of our attention, our love, our piety.

And if anyone else happens to notice, tell them why.

2 Marcus Borg, "Ash Wednesday: Death and Repentance," Day1.org, March 4, 2014, http://day1.org/5706-marcus_borg_ash_wednesday_death_and_repentance.

3 Ibid.

DEVOTIONAL 1

Ash Wednesday

Do the Right Thing

Matthew 3:13–15

Then Jesus came from Galilee to John at the Jordan, to be baptized by him. John would have prevented him, saying, "I need to be baptized by you, and do you come to me?" But Jesus answered him, "Let it be so now; for it is proper for us in this way to fulfill all righteousness." Then he consented.

Irrational Obedience

The very first words of Jesus recorded in the Gospels make absolutely no sense to John the Baptist. Jesus asks John to baptize him. John thinks the idea is ridiculous. He knows who Jesus is. Baptize the Messiah? Unthinkable!

Still, Jesus insists. Just because it is the right thing to do.

Sometimes you may think the things God wants you to do don't make much sense. After all, what's the point of sharing a good word to a total stranger? Or being more deeply involved in your church? Or volunteering with a homeless ministry? Or spending time—even money—helping somebody in need when you don't have much of either?

Today millions of people (including you, I hope) will get a cross-shaped smear of dark ashes on their forehead. That may not make much sense either, but it's designed to remind us that we are dust—human beings destined to die. And that's important to think about as we start the season of Lent and journey with Jesus to the cross, the tomb, and beyond.

When you know the right thing to do, take the risk. Follow John's example of humble yet radical obedience—no questions asked. Then watch what happens. In John's case, a voice sounded from heaven, a dove descended. Wonder what will happen in your case?

» Get Real Why did John have so much trouble with Jesus's request? Have you ever struggled with something God wanted you to do because it didn't make much sense? What happened when you did it anyway?

» Dig In How did John know Jesus? Why did John feel like he needed to be baptized by Jesus, rather than the other way around? Why did Jesus say he needed to be baptized?

» Read On God asked Abram to do something outrageous in Genesis 12:1–4. What was it? Why didn't it make sense? How did Abram respond anyway? Think about how you'd have responded if you had been in Abram's sandals.

» Take Off In prayer, thank God for trusting you enough to shake you up with requests that sometimes don't make sense. Ask God to prepare you to follow the way of Jesus today, no questions asked. And pray for a holy Lent.

Thursday after Ash Wednesday

It's All Very Tempting

Matthew 4:8–11

Again, the devil took him to a very high mountain and showed him all the kingdoms of the world and their splendor; and he said to him, "All these I will give you, if you will fall down and worship me." Jesus said to him, "Away with you, Satan! for it is written, 'Worship the Lord your God, and serve only him.'" Then the devil left him, and suddenly angels came and waited on him.

Taking Down Temptation

It's the War in the Wilderness, Satan versus Jesus, no holds barred. After trying and failing twice to pin Jesus with his tantalizing temptations, the devil tries one last move: He offers Jesus all the world's power and possessions if only he will serve the lord of darkness.

But Jesus will have none of it. Without a moment's hesitation, he orders the evil one away.

Satan offers Jesus the whole world, but Jesus knows what is far more valuable. He knows the truth. He knows who he is and what he's supposed to be about. So he squared up to the temptation with no fear, no weakness, no doubt. Can you do that?

You will face your own temptations. Even today. Remember Jesus's example. Know who you are as God's child, and what you are to be about.

» Get Real How often have you wondered, "If only I were rich. . . if only I could do whatever I wanted . . . if only I could win the lottery . . . "? Jesus could've taken the easy way out here. But he knew it would only lead to destruction. Can you remember a time when you took the easy way out—maybe even doing the right thing but the wrong way or for the wrong reason? What happened? What would you do differently today?

» Dig In Read the first part of this story, Matthew 4:1–7. Jesus was at his weakest physically, but he still stood strong in the face of all the tempter's tricks. How did he respond in each case? What resources did he draw on? What does that tell you about how you can stand against your own temptations?

» Read On Take a look at Hebrews 4:14–16. Why did Jesus have to go through all this temptation in the wilderness? Think about how that helps you relate to him when you face a tempting proposition.

» Take Off Jesus was willing to go through anything for the love of God. He's proven that he wants to give you the strength you need to get through the toughest trials. Ask him for it. Then thank him for his generosity.

DEVOTIONAL 3

Friday after Ash Wednesday

Would You Follow This Man?

Mark 1:16–18

As Jesus passed along the Sea of Galilee, he saw Simon and his brother Andrew casting a net into the sea—for they were fishermen. And Jesus said to them, "Follow me and I will make you fish for people." And immediately they left their nets and followed him.

One Insane Invitation

They were fishermen. Tough. Weather-beaten. Strong. Independent. Smelly. They'd been working hard all night trying to catch fish. Then this stranger walks up to them and invites them to come with him and fish for men and women instead of perch and carp.

What did these tough guys do—laugh him out of town? Throw their catch at him? No. "Immediately they left their nets and followed him."

What was it about Jesus that caused these crusty nuts to lay everything aside to be with him? Was he wearing a nametag that said, "Hello, I'm the Messiah"? Or was his the incredible invitation, which in just a few words offered them friendship, fulfillment, and purpose?

So what's Jesus inviting you to do?

» Get Real What do you think went through the minds of these fishermen when Jesus asked them to join him? How much time did they spend mulling it over? Think about what your own readiness to respond to Jesus is like.

» Dig In Read Mark 1:19–21 and you'll see that the disciples went right to work with Jesus. What exactly was Jesus inviting them to do? Why do you think Jesus wanted these people to join him?

» Read On Luke 5:1–11 has a fuller account of how Jesus met these fishermen. What more does this story tell you about Jesus? And about the fishermen? Can you put yourself in their place and imagine how they might have felt?

» Take Off Jesus was asking a lot of these fishermen. They had to trust him completely, follow him faithfully, listen to him intensely. Spend some time in prayer asking God to make you that kind of follower, too.

⚜

DEVOTIONAL 4

Saturday after Ash Wednesday

What Are You Hungry For?

Matthew 5:1, 2, 6
When Jesus saw the crowds, he went up the mountain; and after he sat down, his disciples came to him. Then he began to speak, and taught them, saying . . . "Blessed are those who hunger and thirst for righteousness, for they will be filled."

Living Thirsty for God
Face it: Some days we just aren't very hungry for doing what's right.

We just want to do things our way. Maybe we're tired, or lazy, or overwhelmed with life, but sometimes our own desires and opinions and pleasures just feel too comfortable to worry about God's.

Maybe today is a day like that for you. Try as you might, you can't make yourself be thirsty for God's presence. If so, recognize it. Admit it. Don't force it. Just let it go for now.

But . . . before you do, ask God as sincerely as you can to increase your appetite for God. To make you hungrier and thirstier for God's presence. Day by day. Moment by moment.

That's a prayer God will love to answer, maybe sooner than you think.

» Get Real God wants our lives to be marked by righteousness— pursuing God, doing what's right and just and authentic. But ask yourself: Do you ever fake it? How does that make you feel? What's going on in your life that you assume you *have* to fake it? What needs to change so that you're genuinely hungry and thirsty for God?

» Dig In Who was Jesus talking to in this "Sermon on the Mount"? It wasn't the religious elite. It was common, ordinary, everyday people who had real lives. People just like us. What does that tell you about who Jesus expects to be living hungry for God?

» Read On Get the big picture of Jesus's message by reading this whole section of the "Sermon on the Mount," Matthew 5:1–12. What else does Jesus want his followers to do? Or to be? How do you stack up? What areas do you need to work on with the Spirit's guidance?

» Take Off So how hungry are you right now? How thirsty would you like to be? Sometimes when you're just making yourself go through the motions of praying and thinking about God, God can bust in and make it all real and alive. Want to try it?

DEVOTIONAL 5

First Sunday in Lent

The Agony of Anger

Matthew 5:22–24

But I say to you that if you are angry with a brother or sister, you will be liable to judgment; and if you insult a brother or sister, you will be liable to the council; and if you say, "You fool," you will be liable to the hell of fire. So when you are offering your gift at the altar, if you remember that your brother or sister has something against you, leave your gift there before the altar and go; first be reconciled to your brother or sister, and then come and offer your gift.

Reeling in Your Resentment

Anger wounds relationships. It hurts everybody involved. In fact, Jesus says anger toward a brother or sister is just as serious as murder (v. 21). That's pretty serious.

Jesus isn't saying to *deny* our angry feelings. He's telling us to *deal* with them positively. If you feel anger toward someone, figure out why. Then go to the person, either to ask for their forgiveness or to talk about it honestly and lovingly. Whatever it takes, work it out. Deal with it— before it becomes deadly.

Jesus says if there's a problem between you and someone else, then there's a problem between you and God. So don't try to put it out of your mind or cover it up. Make peace. Get reconciled. Make it right with them.

By doing so, you're making it right with God.

» Get Real It's not easy to deal with strong emotions like anger, especially if we feel we're right. But Jesus encourages us to take the initiative. Maybe somebody you're angry with came to mind as you read this. An old friend, a family member, a coworker, whoever. What caused the anger you feel? What part did you play in that? How will you reconcile with that person? When?

» Dig In Why do you think it's so important to Jesus that we make peace with somebody we're angry with? What happens to us on the inside when we stay angry with somebody—even if we're right?

» Read On In Ephesians 4:26–27, Paul has some more advice about anger. How do you think this would work in your life, with your own friends and family? When you don't deal with your anger, who wins?

» Take Off Obviously, God cares about our relationships. So think about the important people in your life. Pray for them and thank God for them. Ask God, and yourself, if you're out of sync with any of them. Look for opportunities to express to them personally what they mean to you.

DEVOTIONAL 6

Monday, First Week in Lent

A Natural Outflow

Matthew 6:1–2

Beware of practicing your piety before others in order to be seen by them; for then you have no reward from your Father in heaven. So whenever you give alms, do not sound a trumpet before you, as the hypocrites do in the synagogues and in the streets, so that they may be praised by others. Truly I tell you, they have received their reward.

Why You Do What You Do

You give of your time, concern, love, energy, money. You listen with compassion when a friend calls you to unload. You volunteer with your church group to serve a meal at the homeless shelter. You take a meal to a family because the mother is sick. You give to your church's relief agency.

Why do you do those things? To feel better about yourself? To feel accepted by your friends or other parishioners? To earn praise from important people? To make God love you more?

Or is it the natural outflow of a life in relationship with the One who is all love . . . pure love . . . unlimited love?

Set your sights on living out that kind of love. Make it your goal for today. And go from there.

» Get Real Jesus says if your motives are misplaced, they can undo everything. Think about the last few times you did "good deeds." How did they make you feel? Were they public acts or secret services? So why do you think you really did them? Based on today's text, what might Jesus say to you?

» Dig In What kind of people was Jesus talking about here? What sort of people might they have been in the culture of the day? Who do you think has the hardest time giving with unselfish motives? And why do you think God would care why we do good things?

» Read On Read the next two verses, Matthew 6:3–4. Think through what they tell you about how to give of your money and time—and what God promises you when you do.

» Take Off Join God's Secret Service today. Ask God for an opportunity to help someone in such a way that nobody will know about it except you and God. Be ready to give of your time or money in a way that God would applaud. It might just become a habit.

DEVOTIONAL 7

Tuesday, First Week in Lent

Light in the Darkness

Matthew 6:7–8

When you are praying, do not heap up empty phrases as the Gentiles do; for they think that they will be heard because of their many words. Do not be like them, for your Father knows what you need before you ask him.

God Already Knows

You may not be a person who feels comfortable sharing all your inner stuff with someone else. Perhaps it makes you feel weird that even God knows it. What must God think of you?

But don't let it bother you. Accept it. Relax in it. And look at it for what it is: a promise that God knows everything about you. Every pain you feel. Every unmet need. Every fear. Every salty tear that runs down your face. Every hair you pull out in frustration. In fact, Jesus is saying that God knows lots more about you than even you do.

But if that's true, why should you tell God how you feel and what you need? Because thinking it all through with God in prayer helps you stay totally honest with God. It helps you let go of it all and place it in God's hands. And it opens the door for God to let you know what it is you really need.

» Get Real What are some of the things in your life you hope nobody ever finds out about you? How does it make you feel that God knows all that, and more? How does it make you feel that God loves you completely anyway?

» Dig In Why do you think Jesus didn't approve of babblers of "empty phrases"? What were they trying to do in their prayers? Why would they fail? Who did they really believe in?

» Read On In Psalm 139, the psalmist writes about how God knows him inside and out—and knew it before he was even born. Read that psalm carefully, offering thanks for God's love for you.

» Take Off This may be a good time to do some confessing, bringing some of those dark areas of your soul to light in prayer, either alone or with a priest. Acknowledge the reality that you know that God knows everything about you. Let go of those things from the past and present that you're wrestling with. And accept God's forgiveness, cleansing, and love.

🔱

DEVOTIONAL 8

Wednesday, First Week in Lent

A Living, Breathing Prayer

Matthew 6:9–13

Pray then in this way: Our Father in heaven, hallowed be your name. Your kingdom come. Your will be done, on earth as it is in heaven. Give us this day our daily bread. And forgive us our debts, as we also have forgiven our debtors. And do not bring us to the time of trial, but rescue us from the evil one. [For yours is the kingdom and the power and the glory forever, Amen.]

A Springboard for Conversation

Those words are probably very familiar to you. You may say them every week in church, maybe even every day upon waking or whenever you pray. You may be able to rattle them off without even thinking about them. And that's a problem.

So today, take a good, slow look at those words and think about what they really mean.

Jesus never intended this prayer to be just syllables you memorize so you can pray on autopilot. They're not words carved in stone, mindlessly muttered like some magic formula.

No, this prayer is a living and breathing thing. It's kind of like a "to do" list—a springboard to help you think through and talk over all of life's aspects with God in prayer. Try it.

» Get Real Have you realized how the Lord's Prayer can help you pray? It focuses your prayer on God—who God is and what God does in your life and in the world. It helps you realize how your daily needs are really met. It reminds you that you are forgiven through Christ, and so you should forgive others. It helps you trust God for protection, strength, and wisdom as you face the day. It's all part of a healthy daily prayer life.

» Dig In Did you notice that this entire prayer centers on God the Father, God our heavenly Parent? God is the One who reigns in heaven and on earth—and in your life. Notice that Jesus tells us to pray to "*Our* Father." That means Jesus is right there with you as you pray. This prayer is about you and Jesus entering the presence of God together.

» Read On In Jeremiah 3:19–20 you can catch a glimpse of how God the Father feels when God's children are unfaithful and uncaring. What does that tell you about God your heavenly Father? About God's character? About God's feelings for you?

» Take Off Let the Lord's Prayer be your invitation from Jesus today to worship your heavenly Parent. Offer praise for who God is and what God is doing in your life today. Let this prayer be a springboard for your own intimate conversation with your loving Abba right now.

DEVOTIONAL 9

Thursday, First Week in Lent

Eternal Collectibles

Matthew 6:19–21

Do not store up for yourselves treasures on earth, where moth and rust consume and where thieves break in and steal; but store up for yourselves treasures in heaven, where neither moth nor rust consumes and where thieves do not break in and steal. For where your treasure is, there your heart will be also.

When Possessions Possess You

You can tell you're struggling with materialism when the desire to possess things becomes a primary goal in your life. Every generation has had a problem with materialism. It's just that ours has a lot more stuff to do it with. TVs, apps, malls, and websites overflow with temptations to buy, own, collect, and possess.

But somehow it all fades away in the light of Jesus's words: All that stuff ultimately means nothing.

The flip side of materialism is to focus on "treasures in heaven." They can't be broken, lost, or stolen. They can bring joy and meaning forever and ever.

Where's your heart? What are you pursuing in life? What really makes you feel joyful and fulfilled? The world you live in may have a lot to offer. But just compare it to what God has in store for you. Now, and in the world to come.

» Get Real If you're at home, take a look at all the stuff around you. Clothes, gadgets, furnishings—all the little toys of life. Ask yourself why you own these particular things. Anything here that you just had to have? Are there things you don't have that you're dying to get? Then think again about what Jesus said and consider where your priorities lie.

» Dig In Jesus urges us to collect treasures in heaven. He's certainly not talking about physical objects, so what does he mean? How do you do that? What sorts of things could you do here and now on earth that will lead to treasures in heaven?

» Read On Read Hebrews 13:5. What does it tell you about your attitude toward things? If you're not really satisfied with what you have, you still have far more than the world could ever offer. Because you have God.

» Take Off Make a list of all the stuff you really want right now—maybe the latest cell phone, new outfit, a car, whatever. Then compare each item to what God offers you forever. Talk to God about your attitude about possessions, and ask for strength to keep your focus on heavenly treasures instead of earthly stuff.

DEVOTIONAL 10

Friday, First Week in Lent

Turn Your Light On

Luke 11:34–36

Your eye is the lamp of your body. If your eye is healthy, your whole body is full of light; but if it is not healthy, your body is full of darkness. Therefore consider whether the light in you is not darkness. If then your whole body is full of light, with no part of it in darkness, it will be as full of light as when a lamp gives you light with its rays.

Look into My Eyes

Have you ever looked deeply into someone's eyes? What have you seen? Maybe warm love or bright joy. Perhaps dark pain.

With a little spiritual discernment, you can tell a lot about how a person feels by studying their eyes. They can sparkle or they can be cloudy. They can be alert and open or sleepy and tired. They can be light or dark.

Keep Jesus's words in mind and pay attention to people's eyes today. They may be your friends, family members, maybe even total strangers. Their lips may form a smile, but their eyes may tell you a different story. It could be that you'll have an opportunity to reach out to someone who needs a listening friend. You'll see it in their eyes.

» Get Real Before you look into somebody else's eyes, take a good look at your own in a mirror. What do you see? Do you see light? Is the love of Jesus evident? Or do you have some dark hurt you need to work through with God first? "Therefore consider . . . ."

» Dig In What do your eyes reveal, according to this text? What is this "light" that Jesus is talking about? Where does it come from? What's it supposed to shine on?

» Read On Jesus talked more about "light" in Matthew 5:14–16. How would you tie these two texts together? What are we supposed to do with our light? And why?

» Take Off God wants to clear up your eyes so the divine light of love can shine through them to the whole world. In prayer, apply a few spiritual eye drops. Let God work on those dark areas of your soul—the things that make you sad or scared or guilty. Then let your light shine.

DEVOTIONAL 11

Saturday, First Week in Lent

Don't Worry About It

Luke 12:22–26

He said to his disciples, "Therefore I tell you, do not worry about your life, what you will eat, or about your body, what you will wear. For life is more than food, and the body more than clothing. Consider the ravens: they neither sow nor reap, they have neither storehouse nor barn, and yet God feeds them. Of how much more value are you than the birds! And can any of you by worrying add a single hour to your span of life? If then you are not able to do so small a thing as that, why do you worry about the rest?"

Wasting Your Time in Worry

Life is full of pesky little worries. They chew away at our soul and keep our minds off God. Like that big meeting coming up. Or the report that was due yesterday. Like the friendship that's taking a wrong turn. Or the family member or close friend who's ill or troubled. Or the church ministry to help raise money for. Or loneliness. Take your pick, or add your own.

But when we let these little worries become gigantic and dominate our thoughts, they can overtake our lives and strangle our spiritual freedom.

When we get in that place, it can feel impossible to stop worrying. In fact, Jesus's words can sound awfully simplistic. But that's because his is a simple faith, and worry only succeeds in complicating it.

Life is too much fun, too important, too meaningful, to waste it on worry. Receive Jesus's simple freedom today.

» Get Real Write down the top five things you're worrying about right now (or maybe it's hard to keep it to just five). If Jesus were right here with you, what do you think he would say about your worries? How do you think he can help you let go of them?

» Dig In Who was Jesus speaking to here in Luke 12? Notice the things they worried about—their food and clothes. How often do you worry about things like that? How many people in your community worry about where they will stay or what they will eat? How do your worries compare to theirs? How could you help them?

» Read On Paul offers a powerful antidote for worry in Philippians 4:6–7. What is it? What happens when you take this approach?

» Take Off Jesus said that God provides the birds with everything they need. Then he said, "Of how much more value are you than the birds!" Offer thanks that God promises to meet every need you face—and turn over all those pesky worries to God in faith.

DEVOTIONAL 12

Second Sunday in Lent

The Problem with Judging

Luke 6:41–42

Why do you see the speck in your neighbor's eye, but do not notice the log in your own eye? Or how can you say to your neighbor, "Friend, let me take out the speck in your eye," when you yourself do not see the log in your own eye? You hypocrite, first take the log out of your own eye, and then you will see clearly to take the speck out of your neighbor's eye.

Can't See the Forest for the Logs

Jesus is having a little fun with us. Can you picture this? It's pretty funny—walking around with a log in your eye. It may be slapstick, but it has the sting of truth, too.

Jesus is saying that any time a judgmental thought pops into our head, we ought to grab a mirror. We need to build a habit of taking a good look at our own lives before we start examining someone else's.

That's not easy to do—primarily because with those big logs in our eyes, we're usually blind to our need to deal with our own problems.

But we have to take that log out, because other people need the help we can offer. They've got painful things in their eyes, too, and Jesus wants us to go to our sisters and brothers in love and concern. Log free.

» Get Real It's easy to find fault with somebody else. They don't dress right, look right, believe right, or live right. But notice who has the bigger problem in this passage—a log instead of a speck. Are you blind to your own faults? Have you and God dealt with them?

» Dig In What's a hypocrite? Are there areas in which your beliefs don't match up very well with your actions? How can you avoid being a hypocrite? Will keeping your eyes log free make you too busy to worry so much about the specks in everyone else's?

» Read On Look back at Luke 6:37. What does Jesus tell you there about judging, condemning, and forgiving others? Why is this so important to him? Who's supposed to do the judging?

» Take Off Maybe it's time to do a little log rolling with God. Take care of all that spiritual sawdust clogging your eyes. Talk to God about the thoughts, words, and actions that have made you hypocritical lately. God is ready to forgive you.

DEVOTIONAL 13

Monday, Second Week in Lent

Be a Prayer Pest

Luke 11:9–10

So I say to you, Ask, and it will be given you; search, and you will find; knock, and the door will be opened for you. For everyone who asks receives, and everyone who searches finds, and for everyone who knocks, the door will be opened.

Knocking on Heaven's Door

Nobody likes a nag. But Jesus recognized that persistence does pay off. Sure, God knows what we need and want. But for some reason, God likes it when we ask—and keep asking.

This process of asking, searching, and knocking opens the door for God to enter our hearts and move within us, stimulating growth. If we don't seek God's will in prayer, we may get stuck in our own wants, hyper focused on our own selves.

Of course, Jesus isn't guaranteeing you'll get whatever you ask for, no matter how persistent you are. But if you ask, you'll receive something. It may be the total opposite of what you expect. You may even receive the loss of that particular desire. Or you may receive what you wanted all along—and more.

God knows best. And when we ask for what's best in our lives, God will give it. Abundantly.

» Get Real What have you been asking God for? Strength to overcome a bad habit? Wisdom to make an important decision? A date for Saturday night? Take a look at your requests from God's point of view. And try asking for things you know will bring God pleasure.

» Dig In Read the verses leading up to today's passage, Luke 11:5–8. Jesus gives an example of someone who pesters a friend for something—and gets it despite the hassle. What's the person asking for? Why is he asking for it? What does Jesus say will happen because of this persistence? What does this passage tell you about the verses you read above?

» Read On James 1:5–8 offers insight on one thing you should pray persistently for: wisdom. What does this tell you about God's response? So what attitude should you have in prayer?

» Take Off Maybe you're afraid you're annoying God by asking time and again for the same thing. Far from it. God does something in your heart when you persistently seek what's best. It makes you appreciate God all the more when you realize the answer. So spend some time asking, searching, and knocking with God right now.

DEVOTIONAL 14

Tuesday, Second Week in Lent

How to Get Treated Great

Matthew 7:12

In everything do to others as you would have them do to you; for this is the law and the prophets.

What Do You Want?

What would you like other people to do for you?

You want them to listen to you. To be there when you're under a pile. Have fun with you. Understand you, or at least really try to. Pray for you. Encourage you. Accept you. Warn you when they see you doing something stupid. Give you something special. Spend time with you. Care about you. Surprise you. Open up with you. Respect you. Leave you alone when you need your space. Allow you to be you. Love you.

Wouldn't it be great if all the people in your life did stuff like that for you?

But Jesus wants you to turn it around. If you know how you'd like to be treated, then you know the secret of what others want, too. Instead of waiting for somebody to do something good for you, *you* take the first step. And do that for someone else.

That, Jesus says, is what God's law is all about.

» Get Real It's easy to get our feelings hurt when somebody won't act a certain way or do something we want. But what would happen if, instead of thinking about all the ways you'd like to be treated, you start thinking about all the fun and loving ways you could treat someone else?

» Dig In What does the phrase the "law and the prophets" refer to? Knowing what you do about the Old Testament, does it surprise you that God has always wanted God's people to act with kindness toward each other?

» Read On Paul touched on this idea in Romans 13:8–10. What does he say is the whole point, the big idea, of the law of God? What does this tell you about how you should act toward everybody you run into today?

» Take Off It sounds pretty easy: Love everybody else the way you want to be loved. But you know how hard it is to love certain people. Like who? Pray for God's blessing on them right now. Ask God to give you an opportunity or two today to see how this thing is supposed to work. God will give you everything you need to make it happen—if you ask.

DEVOTIONAL 15

Wednesday, Second Week in Lent

The Touch That Cleans You Up

Mark 1:40–42

A leper came to him begging him, and kneeling he said to him, "If you choose, you can make me clean." Moved with pity, Jesus stretched out his hand and touched him, and said to him, "I do choose. Be made clean!" Immediately the leprosy left him, and he was made clean.

Touching the Untouchable

He was a leper, an outcast of society. His illness made others turn away in disgust and fear. But he approached Jesus—respectfully, even worshipfully—and asked for his healing touch. He knew Jesus had the power.

The law said not to touch a leper. But Jesus did it anyway. He was moved with compassion for the man, and the law of love takes precedence. In that moment, Jesus wanted more than anything for that man to be clean. And immediately the leper was healthy and new, free and alive.

Today, Jesus is still moved with compassion for those who hurt, who are outcasts, who are "unclean" in others' eyes. He wants more than anything to answer prayers for cleansing—physically, emotionally, and spiritually.

Do you need his cleansing? Will you ask him for it? Then maybe you could share the love with an "outcast" you know.

» Get Real Maybe it's something from your past that still eats you up inside. Maybe you just feel like you don't fit in with the crowd. Jesus knows. And he has the power to clean you up from the inside out. What do you need to ask him for today?

» Dig In Find out more about leprosy in a study Bible or Bible dictionary or from an online search. Such skin conditions made people not only physically disabled but also unable to take part in religious ceremonies. What kinds of people might be considered "lepers" by some today?

» Read On In Psalm 25, David asks God to cleanse him from his sins. God delights in doing that. Read this psalm prayerfully and honestly in the presence of God.

» Take Off Once you've experienced God's cleansing, share your joy with somebody else—somebody you know who is avoided, who doesn't quite fit in, who has a background that scares people away. What would you do if they came to you for help? What if you went to them first?

Thursday, Second Week in Lent

Seasick in a Fearful World

Mark 4:35, 37–40

On that day, when evening had come, he said to them, "Let us go across to the other side". . . . A great windstorm arose, and the waves beat into the boat, so that the boat was already being swamped. But he was in the stern, asleep on the cushion; and they woke him up and said to him, "Teacher, do you not care that we are perishing?" He woke up and rebuked the wind, and said to the sea, "Peace! Be still!" Then the wind ceased, and there was a dead calm. He said to them, "Why are you afraid? Have you still no faith?"

Why Fear Makes No Sense

Jesus's disciples were getting hysterical. They were *this close* to drowning in the stormy lake. And Jesus was just sleeping through it—what kind of Savior is that? As it turns out, a powerful one.

It's as though their seemingly valid fear made no sense to Jesus. They had absolutely no reason to be afraid of their circumstances. He was right there with them—what were a few raindrops and lightning bolts to him?

Do you ever hear Jesus asking you why you're so afraid? Why your faith is so weak? People, work, world events, accidents, disasters—there are plenty of reasons to be afraid. But your Savior is not sleeping. He knows all about your fears. And he is ready and willing to calm them.

» Get Real Make a list of the things in your life right now that make your stomach churn and your palms sweat. Which of those things is

Jesus unable to deal with? So why are you so afraid of drowning? Isn't your faith in the same person who quieted the storm?

» Dig In Why do you think Jesus was asleep on the boat? Why did the disciples ask Jesus if he cared about them? In verse 41, what was their response to what happened? Were they still clueless?

» Read On In John 14:27, Jesus promises us peace. It's a different kind of peace than the world gives. How would you compare the two? With Jesus, how can we feel calm even when the world around us is total chaos? How's that possible?

» Take Off Instead of looking at the things that make you frantic, try looking to the one who can calm the storm. Spend some quiet moments with Jesus in prayer. Realize who he is. Understand what he can do in your stormy world. Then let him do it.

🌿

DEVOTIONAL 17

Friday, Second Week in Lent

A Radically New Way of Life

Mark 2:21–22

No one sews a piece of unshrunk cloth on an old cloak; otherwise, the patch pulls away from it, the new from the old, and a worse tear is made. And no one puts new wine into old wineskins; otherwise, the wine will burst the skins, and the wine is lost, and so are the skins; but one puts new wine into fresh wineskins.

Why Don't the Pieces Fit?

Jesus's way is totally new. His is a way of life marked by grace instead of legalism. It's soft and supple like new fabric or leather. It lives and breathes with passion and joy.

But a lifestyle this radical can't be patched onto just any old life. It requires a complete start over. That's why it's useless to try to make Jesus fit into one little compartment of our old way of life. We can't just graft him onto our old systems, habits, and attitudes. That only pulls things apart at the seams, making them worse. The fabric tears, the wine leaks. No, Jesus makes all things new.

If you're struggling with trying to make the old and new pieces fit in your life, give it up. Give God the pieces today. All of them. And God will give you something totally new in return.

» Get Real Are there parts of your old way of life you're trying to make fit into your life with Jesus? Try as you might, they just don't work together. What Jesus offers you is so much better. It's new wine for your soul. It's a life of exhilarating meaning and purpose. So what attitudes or aspects of your life should you let go of?

» Dig In Who is Jesus responding to in this passage? Look at Mark 2:16, 18, 24. What kind of people were the Pharisees? What was their approach to religion all about? How did Jesus differ from them? How did the passage you read today reveal these differences?

» Read On Second Corinthians 5:17 tells us something more about our relationship with God through Jesus. What happens when we believe in him? What does this tell you about the passage from Mark you read today?

» Take Off How have things changed in your life since you became a follower of Jesus? How has he made your life new? What's still old, rigid, and dull in your life? Offer praise for all God has done in your life—and ask God to keep making all things new.

DEVOTIONAL 18

Saturday, Second Week in Lent

The Savior's Surprises

Matthew 9:23–26

When Jesus came to the leader's house and saw the flute players and the crowd making a commotion, he said, "Go away; for the girl is not dead but sleeping." And they laughed at him. But when the crowd had been put outside, he went in and took her by the hand, and the girl got up. And the report of this spread throughout that district.

Unemployed Mourners

Back in Jesus's day, professional mourners were often hired when somebody died. They wept and wailed and played mournful songs. To them it was just a job.

When Jesus arrives at the house where a girl has died, he says something that makes no sense: "The girl is not dead." At that, the mourners laugh and make fun of him. He must be nuts; of course she's dead. They wouldn't have been hired to mourn if she wasn't.

Jesus makes the mourners leave. Then he takes the girl by the hand—and she gets up. Alive.

See, Jesus knows what he's talking about. But too often we get so used to doing things the way we always have, so hardened by our low expectations, so trapped by our small view of life, that we just fall into default mourning mode. What he says really doesn't sink in. We don't take him seriously.

At times like these, Jesus loves to surprise us.

» Get Real The mourners had seen the dead girl. She couldn't be alive. But with Jesus all things are possible. What parts of your life have you given up on? What goal in life seems dead to you? What makes you laugh because it's so ridiculous it could never happen? What could Jesus do about it that would surprise you?

» Dig In When the girl's father went to Jesus for help (v. 18), she was still alive. What happened to keep Jesus from getting there in time (vv. 20–22)? Why didn't that matter to Jesus? What happened as a result of this event (v. 26)?

» Read On The girl's father took a risk coming to Jesus because he was a local official. But his love for his child removed all fear and doubt. His love is a lot like God's love for God's children. Read Psalm 103:11–14 to learn a little more about God's parental love for you.

» Take Off Maybe today Jesus needs to shake up your expectations, stretch your boundaries, end your mourning mode. Will you let him? Talk to him about it. Then see what happens. Surprise!

Third Sunday in Lent

Working the Harvest

Matthew 9:35–38

Then Jesus went about all the cities and villages, teaching in their synagogues, and proclaiming the good news of the kingdom, and curing every disease and every sickness. When he saw the crowds, he had compassion for them, because they were harassed and helpless, like sheep without a shepherd. Then he said to his disciples, "The harvest is plentiful, but the laborers are few; therefore ask the Lord of the harvest to send out laborers into his harvest."

A World of Hurting People

For centuries Jesus's words have inspired believers to give up comfortable lives to spread the good news and work for God's reign in the world. But sometimes we forget why Jesus said these words to his disciples in the first place.

Jesus was traveling from town to town, teaching, ministering, and healing. The crowd that followed him kept growing larger. As he looked at all the people, his heart overflowed with compassion. They were "harassed and helpless." Aimless. Needy.

Know anybody that fits that description today? Just look around. The world is filled with hungry, hurting people. Not just across the world somewhere, but in your own neighborhood, school, or workplace, even your church.

Jesus saw the crowds and had compassion. He sees you, too. Let him love you. Then look around you and share his compassion with all the troubled, harassed, and helpless people you see. You may just be an answer to prayer.

» Get Real Sometimes we get so stuck in our own grinding problems that we feel we can't deal with anybody else's. But a funny thing happens when we try to share Jesus's love with others who need it: It makes our own problems seem a lot smaller than they were. Remember a time you experienced that? What's keeping you from experiencing it again?

» Dig In Read Matthew 9:35 again. Jesus had been very busy, dealing with lots of hurting people. How do you think he felt? Have you ever felt overwhelmed by people? What was he asking the disciples to do in verses 37–38? How do you think God has answered that prayer?

» Read On Read John 4:34–38. What does Jesus tell you there about the "harvest"? What does he mean by "gathering fruit for eternal life"? Does everyone do the same kind of work in the harvest?

» Take Off Do what Jesus asks and pray that God would send workers into the fields of human life. Jesus told the disciples to *pray* for harvesters, and they became the *answer* to that prayer. So open yourself up before God to be an answer to your prayer as well, wherever you are today. And thank God for the privilege of sharing God's love with others.

DEVOTIONAL 20

Monday, Third Week in Lent

Like Serpents and Doves

Matthew 10:1, 16

Then Jesus summoned his twelve disciples and gave them authority over unclean spirits, to cast them out, and to cure every disease and every sickness. . . . "See, I am sending you out like sheep into the midst of wolves; so be wise as serpents and innocent as doves."

Prepared for Anything?

Jesus sends his twelve disciples out into this wolf-filled world with a mission. Not to be sheepish, but to be his cared-for and protected sheep. They have to be prepared for anything: hassles, attacks, injuries, maybe even death. So Jesus gives them some good advice: "Be wise as serpents and innocent as doves."

It sounds strange that Jesus wants us to be like serpents and doves. Those creatures seem to contradict each other. But we need to be like both. He's saying be *innocent*—harmless, sincere, honest. But also be *wise*—shrewd, prepared, aware. It's smart to know how this world operates and to be on your guard. But it's also important not to cause anyone to stumble on their way toward God.

Wise and innocent. Shrewd and harmless. Keep them in balance, and head out into the world.

» Get Real Think of times in your life it would have been helpful to be more like a dove or more like a serpent. Which aspect—harmlessness or shrewdness—is more difficult for you to handle? Which aspect do you need to ask God to help you with?

» Dig In Jesus gave his disciples all kinds of instructions before they went out to serve and minister to others (see Matt. 10:1–15). Why do you think he was so careful to prepare them? What instructions surprise you? How does verse 16 summarize everything Jesus said to them?

» Read On In Acts 20:28–31 Paul warned the leaders of the Ephesian church to care for their flock against the wolves of the world. How serious a situation did they face? How concerned was Paul about it? What did Paul tell them to do?

» Take Off You're going out into your world today. Keep Jesus's words in your mind as you go. Ask God to give you opportunities to put them into action, trusting God for all the wisdom and honesty you need to keep any wolves away.

DEVOTIONAL 21

Tuesday, Third Week in Lent

You Are Worth More

Matthew 10:29–31

Are not two sparrows sold for a penny? Yet not one of them will fall to the ground apart from your Father. And even the hairs of your head are all counted. So do not be afraid; you are of more value than many sparrows.

What Birds Can Teach You

Doesn't God care that your friend seems to be ignoring you? Doesn't God care that you're struggling to finish that important project? Doesn't God care that your job is becoming a huge hassle? Doesn't God care that your family members are fighting? Doesn't God care that you don't have a clue what to do next with your life? Doesn't God care that your loneliness sometimes suffocates you?

Yes. Yes. Yes. Yes. Yes. And forever yes.

Jesus tells us that God knows every hair on our heads. Every ache we feel. Every glimmer of hope that bubbles up. Every fear that gets its hooks into our souls. And God cares about them all.

When life gets tough and painful, that's precisely the time to keep trusting the only One in the universe who has your absolute best interests at heart.

» Get Real God's goal is to see you become all you possibly can be as a human being on earth. Sure, you'll never be perfect—the growth process never stops this side of eternity. And it's often painful and scary. But that's all part of being molded into the image of God's Son. Do you feel that process happening even now?

» Dig In What does Jesus mean about how cheap sparrows are? What does God care about sparrows? What were they used for in the Temple? How do sparrows relate to how much God loves you?

» Read On Read what Jesus said in Luke 21:16–19. How does he hope you'll act? What does he promise you? Is he talking literally or figuratively? So who's ultimately in control—and how does God feel about you?

» Take Off Write down on a piece of paper all those things that are messing up your life right now. Then read today's Scripture again. Give each one of them to God in prayer, knowing that God cares. Then rip up that paper into tiny pieces and throw them away.

DEVOTIONAL 22

Wednesday, Third Week in Lent

The Death That's Really Life

Matthew 10:38–39

And whoever does not take up the cross and follow me is not worthy of me. Those who find their life will lose it, and those who lose their life for my sake will find it.

What's That You're Carrying?

In Jesus's time, criminals were put to death on crosses. When someone in that day looked at a cross, it would be like us looking at an electric chair. Yet Jesus tells us to take up our cross. What does that mean?

It's more than just carrying a burden. It's more than getting your feelings hurt over your beliefs. It's *death*, yet it's *life*. It's being genuinely willing to put your whole life on the line for your faith. And it's the first step to becoming an authentic follower of Jesus.

It's true: Following Jesus requires you to give up your life—your selfish, weak, empty life that's just a shadow of what's possible. Giving that life to God is the way to a far more meaningful life. It's not a life without struggles and pain, but one that offers peace, encouragement, and growth in the midst of all that. It's a life you'll never regret living.

» Get Real How important are the people, activities, hobbies, and responsibilities of your life in light of Jesus? Where does Jesus fit in the mix of who you are? Now you know where he wants to be—so what do you need to give up in order to get there?

» Dig In What does Jesus mean when he says, "Those who find their life will lose it"? What kind of life is that? What kind of life is Jesus offering? What happens when you accept it?

» Read On In Mark 8:34–38 Jesus says more about taking up your cross and following him. What more do you learn there about that process? What are the different end results each way of life brings?

» Take Off Maybe it's someone in your life who is pulling you away from what's important. Maybe it's a habit you know isn't good for your body. Maybe it's a distracting dream to make lots of money. What's keeping you from going all out with Jesus? In a time of honest prayer, let him do a little spiritual surgery on your heart.

🔱

DEVOTIONAL 23

Thursday, Third Week in Lent

Cups of Water and Other Ministries

Matthew 10:40–42

Whoever welcomes you welcomes me, and whoever welcomes me welcomes the one who sent me. Whoever welcomes a prophet in the name of a prophet will receive a prophet's reward; and whoever welcomes a righteous person in the name of a righteous person will receive the reward of the righteous; and whoever gives even a cup of cold water to one of these little ones in the name of a disciple—truly I tell you, none of these will lose their reward.

In the Name of Jesus

Have you ever done something good for someone else just because you are a disciple of Jesus? It's a powerful experience. Even performing a simple act of care in Jesus's name can have huge positive consequences. When we do something for others that expresses our identity as a disciple of Jesus, he is with us. That's powerful, because it not only reveals Jesus's presence with us, but also his willingness to work through our often stubborn, weak, and lazy bodies. When we let Jesus work through us, things happen. Good things.

Is it really that hard to "be Jesus" to somebody in need? A cup of cold water. A listening ear and an open heart. A hug. Simple ways to share Jesus's love with a needy soul. They're things even you can do.

» Get Real How would you rate your readiness? When you see someone who needs help, do you glance away and act like you didn't see them? Or are you quick to reach out to them in Jesus's name? Think of times you've reacted both ways. Ask yourself why you acted the way you did—and what happened within you.

» Dig In The whole passage today is about welcoming, serving, and helping. And in each case Jesus promises a reward. What kind of reward is he talking about? What kind of attitude do we need to be sensitive to these opportunities? For an authentic and passionate disciple, how hard is it?

» Read On This same encouragement to serve is expressed in Proverbs 14:31 and 19:17. When you help someone in need, you're really serving God. What do these two verses add to your understanding of the concept?

» Take Off Sometimes when you look at the world through your own eyes, you can come up with good reasons not to get involved. Just mind your own business. Let somebody else do it. But when you look at the world through Jesus's eyes, you might see a thirsty child. Ask God to give you righteous eyesight today, and you'll see needs everywhere you look.

DEVOTIONAL 24

Friday, Third Week in Lent

Take a Load Off

Matthew 11:28–30

Come to me, all you that are weary and are carrying heavy burdens, and I will give you rest. Take my yoke upon you, and learn from me; for I am gentle and humble in heart, and you will find rest for your souls. For my yoke is easy, and my burden is light.

A Bondage That Sets Free

Life can be so busy. Work assignments, church group meetings, chores, family stuff, unexpected emergencies—it just never ends. And when you stop for a moment to catch your breath, you realize how wiped out you are, how burdened by all the responsibility you carry—and how fearful, frustrated, and angry you can get about it all.

That's when you need to hear Jesus. He's saying, "Come here, beloved. Come be with me. Let me take all those burdens off your aching back. Put your feet up. Rest. And let's talk."

Jesus invites you to exchange your burdens—the loads of responsibility, fear, old hurts given and received—and exchange them for his easy yoke. Join him, so you can know him more intimately, learn about life from him, live in fellowship with him.

Yes, there is a price for accepting his rest: You are yoked, bound to him. Connected forever. But it's a bondage that is freeing, because the heavy, painful burdens you're used to carrying are lifted away into his care.

» Get Real Everybody has responsibilities in life, but there may be some burdens you're carrying that you need to give up. Like the hurtful act you committed that God has already forgiven. Like your fears about the future. Like the self-centered dreams you know aren't God's best for you. What burdens do you need to give to Jesus?

» Dig In What exactly is a "yoke"? How was it used? What's the picture Jesus is drawing here? Can you think of a modern-day equivalent to the yoke of Jesus's day?

» Read On Read 1 John 5:2–5 and get some more insight into whether or not God's way of life really is as burdensome as it feels sometimes— or as some people say it is. What happens when we love God this way? How well have you been "conquering the world" lately?

» Take Off Can you hear Jesus? He's still speaking that invitation to you. Got a few minutes? Take him up on his offer. Rest with him. Let him love you. Then put on that easy yoke of his before you head out for the day.

⚜

DEVOTIONAL 25

Saturday, Third Week in Lent

Overflowing with Goodness

Matthew 12:33–35

Either make the tree good, and its fruit good; or make the tree bad, and its fruit bad; for the tree is known by its fruit. You brood of vipers! How can you speak good things, when you are evil? For out of the abundance of the heart the mouth speaks. The good person brings good things out of a good treasure, and the evil person brings evil things out of an evil treasure.

Your Words Reveal Your Heart

You probably know people who always cheer you up. Their conversation just oozes encouragement and wisdom. When you spend time with them, you always leave full of joy and warmed by love.

Other people may affect you totally differently. Their conversation focuses on themselves. Their problems. How life is so unfair. How people have hurt them. Spending time with people like that can leave you emotionally and even physically drained. But God can change even them.

What comes out of a person's mouth reveals what's happening inside. So what are you storing up in your heart? Jesus says there's an easy way to find out: Pay attention to your conversation. Let God fill up your heart with good things, and your conversation can be a blessing to others.

» Get Real Have you paid attention to your own words lately? Are they positive or negative? Do they build up or tear down? Jesus isn't saying be insincere. But he is telling you to listen to what you're saying because it shows what's in your heart.

» Dig In According to Matthew 12:24, who is Jesus answering? Who are the "brood of vipers" and what does that mean? What was Jesus saying about his own actions in healing the demon-possessed man (v. 22)?

» Read On Check out these proverbs that shine more light on your words and your heart: Proverbs 10:11; 12:14; 22:11; 25:11; 26:24–26. What do they add to your understanding of Jesus's words?

» Take Off Take some time with God to examine your heart—and then keep a check on your conversation throughout the day to see how you're doing. Ask God to fill your heart with good stuff . . . and let it overflow to others.

DEVOTIONAL 26

Fourth Sunday in Lent

Your Forever Family

Matthew 12:47–50

Someone told him, "Look, your mother and your brothers are standing outside, wanting to speak to you." But to the one who had told him this, Jesus replied, "Who is my mother, and who are my brothers?" And pointing to his disciples, he said, "Here are my mother and my brothers! For whoever does the will of my Father in heaven is my brother and sister and mother."

Getting to Know Your Family

Jesus was teaching the crowds when somebody slipped a note to him: His mother and brothers were waiting. They wanted to speak to him. But Jesus's response probably startled the person who gave him the message. "Who is my mother, and who are my brothers? These people here—they're my mother and my brothers!"

Jesus wasn't denying his earthly family, acting as though they didn't exist. He was actually broadening his family circle to include spiritual relationships. And whoever genuinely follows him, whoever does God's will, is part of his forever family.

It's a family just as important as your natural, physical family. A family you can grow in, get supported by, share with, and love forever.

» Get Real So who's in your spiritual family? How strong are the bonds in the spiritual family you're a part of—your church group, prayer or Bible study group, or fellowship bunch? Are you working on building strong relationships with other siblings in Jesus—including those outside your circle of comfort?

» Dig In Ever wonder what Mary and her other sons wanted to talk to Jesus about? Skim through the first part of Matthew 12 and note some of the things going on. Do you think they were worried about Jesus? Doubtful? Frightened?

» Read On Catch a glimpse in Psalm 133 of what God has in mind for sisters and brothers living together in unity. It's a beautiful picture. How does it compare to your own relationships in the faith?

» Take Off Do something special for one of your spiritual sisters or brothers today as a way of thanking them for their love and support in your life. And if you're having trouble thinking of who that might be, pray about it, think of someone, and arrange to get together sometime to talk, pray, or just get to know each other. It could be the first step in a fulfilling spiritual family relationship.

DEVOTIONAL 27

Monday, Fourth Week in Lent

The Ultimately Blessed

Luke 10:23–24

Then turning to the disciples, Jesus said to them privately, "Blessed are the eyes that see what you see! For I tell you that many prophets and kings desired to see what you see, but did not see it, and to hear what you hear, but did not hear it."

What Was It Like to Be with Jesus?

It's natural to be a little envious of Jesus's disciples. Imagine sitting around him listening to his radical teachings. Witnessing him touch and heal broken bodies and hearts. Walking with him from town to town, never quite knowing what to expect. Amazing. They were deeply blessed because they had experiences that righteous prophets and kings of the past yearned to have.

We can look back on those days with a little envy and a lot of awe, wondering what it must have been like to be part of the crowd that followed Jesus. But the truth is, you're even more blessed than they were. Because Jesus's spirit dwells within you.

Think about that. There's no need to be just a part of a huge crowd, straining to see and hear him from a distance. Jesus is with you. In you. Around you. Under you. Above you. Beside you.

Blessed are *you.*

» Get Real Sometimes we think of Jesus as just a historical character who lived a long time ago in a land far away. But he's even closer to you than he was to the disciples. How does that make you feel today? Comforted? Empowered? A little scared? Guilty? Think about why you feel the way you do.

» Dig In Look through the first part of Luke 10 to get the setting for this passage. Who's here? What's going on? Then note verse 23 again. What's Jesus doing here? How do you think the disciples felt about what he was saying?

» Read On Spend some time reading 1 Peter 1:20–23. Peter talks about how the prophets looked forward to the blessings *you* would enjoy as a faithful Christian. Who were they serving, and what did they experience? If you saw this on a timeline, where would the prophets be? Jesus during his time on earth? You?

» Take Off The disciples had nothing on you. Sure, they got to laugh and walk and talk and be with Jesus. But so can you—in even more intimate ways. Let that thought get you started in a time of prayer, conversing with Jesus as though he were right there with you. He is.

Tuesday, Fourth Week in Lent

Permeating the World

Luke 13:20–21

And again he said, "To what should I compare the kingdom of God? It is like yeast that a woman took and mixed in with three measures of flour until all of it was leavened."

In the Kitchen with Jesus

Jesus loved to teach by telling stories. He used lots of illustrations to help his followers understand the concept of the reign of God, the way of Christ. But what's he talking about here? Is he just sharing recipes?

Hardly. He's saying believers are supposed to be like yeast in the world. A bit of yeast hidden in a big batch of flour eventually works through the whole thing. The yeast makes the flour rise when it's baked. Without it, bread is flat and hard.

That's the way the realm of God is designed to work on earth: Believers living and working in the world. Permeating it. Influencing it. Making it rise. So that its righteous influence spreads and builds and grows, penetrating society and transforming one life after another. It's a process that will continue slowly but surely until the end of time.

Wherever you go today, be like yeast. Not dramatic or overpowering, but simple and steady in your faith.

» Get Real What kind of influence are you having in your world? What little deeds and simple words are you sharing with your friends, neighbors, at work, or wherever you go, that help influence the world positively? What part are you playing in the realm of God on earth?

» Dig In Think about this woman Jesus is talking about. How much work would be involved to make sure the yeast is spread evenly throughout 50 pounds of flour? What does that tell you about the process of living and sharing the way of Jesus in the world?

» Read On In 1 Corinthians 5:6–8, Paul talks about two different kinds of yeast—old yeast that influences for bad, and new yeast that makes authentic, wholesome bread. What does this add to your understanding of the effect of righteous yeast in the world?

» Take Off It's often the little things we do and say that ultimately result in greater impact over time. Ask God to keep that truth in mind today as you go out into a world that needs God's touch.

DEVOTIONAL 29

Wednesday, Fourth Week in Lent

Let Jesus Be Jesus

Mark 6:2–4

On the sabbath he began to teach in the synagogue, and many who heard him were astounded. They said, "Where did this man get all this? What is this wisdom that has been given to him? What deeds of power are being done by his hands! Is not this the carpenter, the son of Mary and brother of James and Joses and Judas and Simon, and are not his sisters here with us?" And they took offense at him. Then Jesus said to them, "Prophets are not without honor, except in their hometown, and among their own kin, and in their own house."

Who Does He Think He Is?

Jesus goes home to Nazareth. Home to the people who knew him as a boy, people who thought they knew who Jesus really was. And their reaction to him? "Who does he think he is? Where does he get off claiming to say and do such things? We know who he really is."

Jesus offended them by shattering their assumptions about what he should do or be. Jesus wasn't able to perform many miracles in their midst (see vv. 5–6). They robbed themselves of the blessing of a lifetime because of their doubts and small-minded judgmentalism.

Before you judge them too harshly, consider this: Maybe your small-minded assumptions of who Jesus is are keeping him boxed up in your life, powerless to help you deal with your doubts, fears, troubles, and questions. Could that explain the lack of the miraculous in your life today? Let Jesus be Jesus and see what happens.

» Get Real Have you ever thought—consciously or subconsciously—that Jesus really wouldn't want to get involved in your problems? Or that he's not all that interested in your future? How are those thoughts any different than those of Jesus's hometown folks? Does he need to shatter some of your assumptions, too?

» Dig In In some ways, how do the statements of the townspeople make sense? What does that tell you about Jesus growing up? How do you think the disciples felt about how Jesus was treated?

» Read On Read Mark 6:5–6 to see what happened as a result of the townspeople's unbelief. How did Jesus feel about the situation? Why do you think he felt that way?

» Take Off To really get to know Jesus, plan on spending time each day beyond Lent reading and meditating on the Gospels. Use the Daily Office lectionary or a devotional booklet. And talk with him in prayer as though he were right there with you, listening, caring, loving you. Because he is.

DEVOTIONAL 30

Thursday, Fourth Week in Lent

That Risky First Step

Matthew 14:15–16

When it was evening, the disciples came to him and said, "This is a deserted place, and the hour is now late; send the crowds away so that they may go into the villages and buy food for themselves." Jesus said to them, "They need not go away; you give them something to eat."

A Picnic for Thousands

Jesus is mourning the murder of his cousin and friend, John the Baptist. He just wants to get away, to grieve in private. But the crowds keep following him. Surrounding him. Needing him. Of course, he has compassion on them and spends the rest of the day healing many of them.

As the skies grow dark, Jesus's disciples thoughtfully suggest he send everybody home so they can get food before nightfall. No, Jesus says, "You give them something to eat."

"Us?" they must have yelped in shock. "Are you kidding? We've only got five loaves of bread and two fish here, and there must be thousands of people."

But you know the rest of the story. Jesus blesses that little snack, and after everybody eats they still have baskets full of leftovers.

Day after day, we ask Jesus to fix things, give us things, do things for us. Maybe today he's saying, "You do it." He just may take your risky first step, bless it, and multiply its impact.

» Get Real Ever think what Jesus is asking of you is crazy? What has God been nudging you to do lately that seems impossible? What would happen if you took that risky first step of obedience? How might God bless your heartfelt effort?

» Dig In It always helps to read the whole context when studying a Scripture text. So read through Matthew 14:1–21 and get the big picture. How does John's murder color your understanding of what was going on with the crowds?

» Read On After this eventful day, Jesus finally did get away to pray (see Matt. 14:22–23). When you get stressed out or tired or upset about something, what does this tell you about taking care of yourself?

» Take Off You look around and see needs everywhere. Hurting friends, sick relatives, people who need help. But you only have a little to share. Let Jesus bless that and use it. That's the stuff of miracles.

Friday, Fourth Week in Lent

Outrageous Obedience, Deadening Doubt

Matthew 14:28–31

Peter answered him, "Lord, if it is you, command me to come to you on the water." He said, "Come." So Peter got out of the boat, started walking on the water, and came toward Jesus. But when he noticed the strong wind, he became frightened, and beginning to sink, he cried out, "Lord, save me!" Jesus immediately reached out his hand and caught him, saying to him, "You of little faith, why did you doubt?"

In Over Your Head

In the middle of a dark night, the disciples find themselves in a small boat trying to survive a battle with a stormy lake. They aren't doing very well. But Jesus walks out to them—on the water—to help.

Peter must have thought that looked like fun because he asks to walk on the water too. Jesus says, "Come on," and Peter steps out—though it turns out to be a short walk. The brisk winds scare him and he begins to sink into the sea. Fear and doubt rob him of an experience of a lifetime. He lets his scary circumstances get to him—and he looks away from Jesus.

"Why did you doubt?" Jesus's words must have burned into Peter's soul. Just think what could happen if Jesus didn't have to ask you the same question.

» Get Real It is pretty scary out there, isn't it? You might not be in the middle of a storm on a lake, but life itself can get stormy, distracting you from following Jesus wherever he beckons. So what blessings are you letting your fear or doubt smother?

» Dig In Why did Peter say, "Lord, if it is you . . . "? Look back at verse 26. That means Peter was really being courageous. Why do you think he changed so quickly? When he started sinking, what did he do? What do you learn about Peter and Jesus from this passage?

» Read On Read the next few verses to find out what happened after Peter and Jesus got in the boat. What did the disciples say and do? Why were they so impressed with Jesus?

» Take Off Let God show you the boat you're in. And the waves around you. And the storm that's brewing. And the Savior that's standing just a few waves away from you, beckoning you to "Come!" What will you do? Talk to him about it.

DEVOTIONAL 32

Saturday, Fourth Week in Lent

Right Things, Wrong Reasons

Mark 7:14–16

Then he called the crowd again and said to them, "Listen to me, all of you, and understand: There is nothing outside a person that by going in can defile, but the things that come out are what defile."

Do You Have a Heart Condition?

Jesus had been verbally wrestling with the Pharisees, the religious leaders who seemed to do all the right things for all the wrong reasons. Then he told the crowd this simple statement—and in the process really burned the Pharisees.

Jesus knew they may have been ultra-careful about the food they put into their mouths—and they were sure to wash their hands first. But that was totally insignificant in light of understanding and controlling what came out of their mouths. Their words reflected what was really in their hearts.

See, the specific ways you live your life don't really matter if there's no heart behind them. Instead of just taking care of the surface details of obeying God, you have to deal with your heart—your spiritual reality. And the way to check your heart is to pay attention to what comes out of it.

» Get Real It's really a question of motives, isn't it? Are you doing all the right things as a follower of Christ—but for all the wrong reasons? Trying to look good, be accepted by your peers, make God love you more? Why do you do what you do as a follower of Jesus or a member of your church? That takes a deep examination of your heart.

» Dig In Why do you think Jesus summoned the whole crowd to listen at this point? What does "defile" mean? How serious a problem is it if you're defiled, and what can you do about it?

» Read On Jesus had to further explain to his disciples what he meant. Read Mark 7:17–23. How do one's actions reveal what's going on in one's heart? How does Jesus's slightly exasperated explanation here help you understand the big idea he's trying to get across?

» Take Off If you have to deal with some of the negative behavior Jesus listed (vv. 21–23), it's time to pray about it and accept God's forgiveness. If you have to come to grips with the right things you do for the wrong reasons, guess what—it's also time to pray about it and accept God's forgiveness.

Fifth Sunday in Lent

Who Do You Say He Is?

Luke 9:18–20

Once when Jesus was praying alone, with only the disciples near him, he asked them, "Who do the crowds say that I am?" They answered, "John the Baptist; but others, Elijah; and still others, that one of the ancient prophets has arisen." He said to them, "But who do you say that I am?" Peter answered, "The Messiah of God."

What's the Buzz?

While he is praying, a question arises in Jesus's mind: Who do people think he is? What's the buzz about him?

People are certainly talking. And his disciples report what they've heard—all kinds of rumors about who Jesus might be, some prophet or other come back to life.

But then Jesus puts the question directly to his companions: "But who do you say that I am?" Imagine their surprise. After all, they were always hanging out with Jesus. Who would know him better? Why would he ask them a question like that? Is he curious about their thinking? Is he testing them? Maybe. But the question still hangs in the air: "Who do you say that I am?"

What do you tell others about Jesus? And what does the way you live your life tell others about Jesus? The answers to those questions will answer Jesus's question for you today.

» Get Real You may know a lot about Jesus. You've heard all the stories in church. You read the Gospels. But take a moment to ask yourself: Who do you say he is? What difference is he making in your life? How does he shine through you to others?

» Dig In Why do you think Jesus was thinking about this question? What was he doing when he asked the disciples? Do you think all the disciples really understood who Jesus was and what he was doing on the earth?

» Read On Matthew 16:13–20 offers a different account of what happened. What was Jesus's reaction to Peter's declaration that he was the Messiah? How does this passage help you understand why Jesus was asking his companions this question?

» Take Off Spend a few minutes thinking about Peter's answer: "You are the Messiah, the Son of the living God" (Matt. 16:16). Prayerfully consider each word, what it means, and how it impacts your life.

DEVOTIONAL 34

Monday, Fifth Week in Lent

Mountain-Moving Faith

Matthew 17:19–20

Then the disciples came to Jesus privately and said, "Why could we not cast it out?" He said to them, "Because of your little faith. For truly I tell you, if you have faith the size of a mustard seed, you will say to this mountain, 'Move from here to there,' and it will move; and nothing will be impossible for you."

Something's Missing Here

The disciples had blown it. A man had asked them to help his demon-possessed son, and they couldn't. What went wrong?

Jesus explained that if the disciples had even the tiniest bit of faith—faith the size of a mustard seed—they could move a mountain. In fact, with authentic faith they could do anything.

So is it that hard to have such a small amount of faith in this world?

It may not be God's will for you to move a mountain. It may be enough for you to just move your feet in a certain direction, to reach out with your hands, to speak a word of hope, to open your heart to someone outside your comfort zone. Even those simple efforts require great faith at times.

Today, have faith. It may not be as big as a mustard seed, but it'll be a start.

» Get Real Nothing is impossible. Jesus said so. So what gigantic efforts are you avoiding even trying because you don't think they can be done? And what little steps are you afraid to take because you might fail?

» Dig In What's a mustard seed? Look it up in a Bible dictionary or search online. So what does that add to your understanding of what Jesus means?

» Read On Read the previous verses, Matthew 17:14–18. What do you learn about the boy's father? Why do you think Jesus reacted the way he did? How do you think the disciples felt about the whole thing—could they have learned something important?

» Take Off So how big is your faith? How big do you want it to be? How do you think you can make your faith grow? Jesus would love to talk it over with you.

DEVOTIONAL 35

Tuesday, Fifth Week in Lent
Restoring a Broken Friendship

Matthew 18:15

Jesus said, "If another member of the church sins against you, go and point out the fault when the two of you are alone. If the member listens to you, you have regained that one."

How to Heal a Hurting Relationship

Here's Jesus's advice on how to heal a broken relationship. If a friend hurts you, don't bottle it up inside. Don't complain to somebody else about it. Don't mope over it. Instead, go and tell them how you feel.

Of course, what they do with the matter is up to them. They may ignore it, deny it, or fight even harder against you. But Jesus says if your brother or sister listens to you, you've won them back. Your relationship is restored the way it's supposed to be—open and honest and mutually supporting. Few things on earth are sweeter than that.

The hard part is taking Jesus at his word—actually going to someone and telling them how they hurt you. But maybe Jesus's word today will give you the push you need to go do that. Worst case, nothing changes. Best case, you've got your brother or sister back in your life. That makes it worth every effort you can make.

» Get Real So who is it? Who's the friend, the church member, the family member that you're worked up about? Somebody who said something or did something that really hurt you? How are you handling it so far? What are you going to do about it? And one more thing—what happens if somebody comes to you because you've hurt them?

» Dig In Pay particular attention to the words Jesus uses. The Greek word for "church member" is technically "brother"—a close sibling in the faith. Go "alone"—don't make a public case about it; keep it between the two of you. "Regained"—what's the alternative?

» Read On Jesus goes on to give more instruction on handling broken relationships in Matthew 18:16–17. So there are specific steps you should take if you can't get the problem resolved between the two of you. How would that look in your case? What would you do?

» Take Off Relationships are vital to a whole life. When they're in bad shape, they can really hurt. When they're working well, there's nothing better. Consider with Jesus in prayer the various relationships in your life. Ask God for wisdom to handle them with care.

DEVOTIONAL 36

Wednesday, Fifth Week in Lent

What's Controlling You?

Mark 10:17–22

As he was setting out on a journey, a man ran up and knelt before him, and asked him, "Good Teacher, what must I do to inherit eternal life?" Jesus said to him, "You know the commandments: 'You shall not murder; You shall not commit adultery; You shall not steal; You shall not bear false witness; You shall not defraud; Honor your father and mother.'" He said to him, "Teacher, I have kept all these since my youth." Jesus, looking at him, loved him and said, "You lack one thing; go, sell what you own, and give the money to the poor, and you will have treasure in heaven; then come, follow me." When he heard this, he was shocked and went away grieving, for he had many possessions.

Stunned by Jesus's Words

The young man seemed eager to enter God's realm. He had obeyed God's laws all his life. What else did he have to do?

Jesus gazed into his eyes with love, then answered with simple yet stunning words that hit the young man where it really hurt: his wallet. He walked away distraught, knowing that he couldn't let go of the things that controlled him—his money and possessions.

Does Jesus expect all of his followers to sell off everything, as he asked this man? Or did he realize that this young person, despite the fact that he claimed to obey the Law, had actually made money his god—and he could never fully worship the real God because he was too busy worshiping his possessions?

Anything in our lives that hinders our freedom to serve God should be set aside. That's when we will receive the treasure of heaven.

» **Get Real** Are there things in your life you just have to have—maybe friends, or wealth, or fame, or whatever? If you went up to Jesus and asked him what you needed to do to enter the realm of God, what do you think he'd tell you? What would his loving gaze reveal? And how would you respond?

» **Dig In** Be sure to read the whole passage, Mark 10:17–31. Note Jesus's initial reaction to the man's question. What did he mean in verse 18? Notice also verse 21: "Jesus, looking at him, loved him." Jesus had compassion on him and knew how trapped he was by his wealth. What does that tell you about Jesus?

» Read On Keep reading in Mark 10:24–27. How did this disciple react to what Jesus said? How does Jesus's answer in verse 27 help you put the whole matter into context?

» Take Off Give it to God. Whatever's holding you back or keeping you trapped, whatever you're putting your trust and your hope in, let go. Let God have it. And let yourself fall wholly into God's hands.

DEVOTIONAL 37

Thursday, Fifth Week in Lent

One Awesome Servant

Mark 10:42–45

So Jesus called them and said to them, "You know that among the Gentiles those whom they recognize as their rulers lord it over them, and their great ones are tyrants over them. But it is not so among you; but whoever wishes to become great among you must be your servant, and whoever wishes to be first among you must be slave of all. For the Son of Man came not to be served but to serve, and to give his life a ransom for many."

Hanging Out in the Servant 'Hood

Jesus is the co-creator of the universe. Sovereign over everything. The one who possesses all wisdom and honor and power and glory. By all rights, he should be served as we would a monarch of the realm.

But that's not the way of God. God is not coercive, demanding our attention and our fealty. God does not "lord it over" us. God is no tyrant. Why do so many earthly rulers get it so wrong?

Jesus set the example of God's way of leading: He set all that aside and came to live without any expectation of being served, but with every intention of serving others. That's not an easy attitude to have. Too often, even when we serve others, we do so with ulterior motives.

True servanthood is a choice, freely made, freely lived. Is it your choice?

» Get Real So how's your servant attitude? What would your life look like if you became a willing servant to others? Your friends, your colleagues, your neighbors, your family members?

» Dig In The Jews of Jesus's time lived under the harsh rule of the Roman authorities. Jesus says they were going after greatness the wrong way. According to this passage, what does a true leader look like? How optional is this attitude, according to Jesus?

» Read On In Galatians 5:13–15, Paul talks about how this servanthood thing is supposed to work among Christians. How does he help you understand what your attitude should be toward others?

» Take Off We're surrounded by a culture that's all about "me." My rights. What people owe me. So Jesus's words can be a bit off-putting, even overwhelming. Spend some time in prayer with him considering how it's supposed to work in your life.

DEVOTIONAL 38

Friday, Fifth Week in Lent

Righteous Rage

Mark 11:15–17

Then they came to Jerusalem. And he entered the temple and began to drive out those who were selling and those who were buying in the temple, and he overturned the tables of the money changers and the seats of those who sold doves; and he would not allow anyone to carry anything through the temple. He was teaching and saying, "Is it not written, 'My house shall be called a house of prayer for all the nations'? But you have made it a den of robbers."

Jesus Hits His Limit

The temple, God's house, had become a mini-mall. Vendors set up shop to sell doves, exchange money unfairly, and offer all sorts of religious goods to those who came to worship God. And they cheated them in the process.

God's temple had become a sham and a scam. The leaders bled people dry in the name of God. If they were to fulfill their religious duties, the people had no choice but to deal with these frauds.

And it made Jesus mad. Righteously enraged, he careened through the temple turning over tables, setting loose the sacrificial animals, spilling coins in every direction. It must have been a wild sight to witness.

Jesus's convictions were unshakable and he didn't hesitate to act on them. There's a time to be angry, a place to show anger, and a way to resolve anger. Let Jesus be your model.

» Get Real What's your reaction to this story? Can you see yourself acting in righteous anger as Jesus did? Or does it scare you? Maybe there's a situation you know about where God's justice is not being served. What could you and others in your church do about it?

» Dig In How soon after Jesus arrived in Jerusalem did this incident happen? How important was this situation to him? What passages did he quote to those in the temple, and why?

» Read On The next verse (Mark 11:18) reveals the response of the religious leaders. How would you characterize them? What had to be going through their minds at this point? What did the people think of Jesus?

» Take Off Jesus saw an unjust situation and took action. It was action appropriate to the need. Think through this incident in prayer, asking God to give you wisdom and strength to stand firm on your convictions—and take action to bring about justice in God's will.

🔱

DEVOTIONAL 39

Saturday, Fifth Week in Lent
Honoring Your Responsibilities

Matthew 22:18–22

But Jesus, aware of [the Pharisees'] malice, said, "Why are you putting me to the test, you hypocrites? Show me the coin used for the tax." And they brought him a denarius. Then he said to them, "Whose head is this, and whose title?" They answered, "The emperor's." Then he said to them, "Give therefore to the emperor the things that are the emperor's, and to God the things that are God's." When they heard this, they were amazed; and they left him and went away.

An Attempted "Gotcha"

The Pharisees were trying to paint Jesus into a corner, forcing him to say something he'd get in trouble over. They asked him a no-win question: "What do you think—is it lawful to pay taxes to Caesar, or not?"

If Jesus said yes, the people would be angry with him because they hated Roman rule. But if he said no, the Romans could arrest him for trying to cause a rebellion.

Of course, Jesus saw right through their trick. He explained that members of God's realm have a dual responsibility. We're obligated to support the government, which is intended to provide for the welfare of the people. But above all, we're obligated to God and God's realm.

Honor your responsibilities—paying whatever you owe to whomever it's due. But always remember whose will comes first.

» Get Real So what are your civic responsibilities? How do you view your local, state/province, and national governments, and the part you play in them? How do your views fit into what Jesus teaches here?

» Dig In Look back at Matthew 22:15 and you'll see that the Pharisees purposely tried to trap Jesus. And verse 16 reveals how they tried to fool him by praising him. How do you think Jesus saw right through them? And how did they respond to him?

» Read On Following the Pharisees' attempt, here come the Sadducees in verses 23–33. How did they approach Jesus? How did he respond to their tricky question? And how did the people react this time?

» Take Off We live in a world that's full of responsibilities and duties. And it's easy to let God get lost in all that. Our job or school or family create so many demands on our time and energy. So where are you right now in making God the number one priority of your life?

DEVOTIONAL 40

Palm Sunday

Shouting Stones

Luke 19:37–40

As he was now approaching the path down from the Mount of Olives, the whole multitude of the disciples began to praise God joyfully with a loud voice for all the deeds of power that they had seen, saying, "Blessed is the king who comes in the name of the Lord! Peace in heaven, and glory in the highest heaven!" Some of the Pharisees in the crowd said to him, "Teacher, order your disciples to stop." He answered, "I tell you, if these were silent, the stones would shout out."

What's Stopping You?

This is when it all starts. The week ahead will be marked by every emotion imaginable—from joy to grief, from love to fear—as we make our way to the cross. Jesus takes the path down the Mount of Olives on a borrowed colt and receives the raucous praise of a whole multitude of followers.

Did they have any idea what they were getting into?

They "praise God joyfully with a loud voice," blessing Jesus along the way to the city and his destiny. And of course, this upsets the hypocritical, self-protecting Pharisees, who urge him to make his disciples shut up. But he refuses. The praise of God, the lively witness to who Jesus is, simply cannot be stopped—even the stones would shout.

So as we enter this week, ask yourself, what's stopping me from praising God, from telling someone about Jesus? Carry a small rock in your pocket or purse today to remind you to offer praise.

» Get Real Have you ever had such good news you felt you would burst unless you shared it with someone? Jesus indicates here that all of creation has that same urge—the unstoppable desire to praise God and proclaim God's way. So why are you so reticent to join in?

» Dig In Read the whole story of Palm Sunday in Luke 19:28–40. What do you make of the preparations for this entry into Jerusalem— borrowing the colt? Do some digging in a commentary or online about what the symbolism of riding the colt might mean.

» Read On Read the next few verses, Luke 19:41–44. What happens next? Why does Jesus weep over the city before entering it? What does this emotional response tell you about Jesus?

» Take Off Many churches today will observe Passion Sunday, using the lengthy liturgy of the Passion. We'll be moving through the events of Holy Week in the days ahead, so for now, put yourself with the disciples following Jesus on the way to Jerusalem, shouting praises to God, proclaiming Jesus as God's Son. Knowing what's to come, how do you feel? How do you respond?

⚜

DEVOTIONAL 41

Monday in Holy Week

The One True Father

Matthew 23:8–10

But you are not to be called rabbi, for you have one teacher, and you are all students. And call no one your father on earth, for you have one Father—the one in heaven. Nor are you to be called instructors, for you have one instructor, the Messiah.

Waiting with Outstretched Arms

Jesus makes a strong case against the prideful Pharisees who love to be first, lording it over the common people. Jesus's followers are not to be that way. We're all siblings.

As he challenges his listeners, Jesus helps us keep in mind a fundamental fact: There really is only one Father, one heavenly Parent. God. Our Abba.

Sure, you have or had an earthly father. But Jesus is pointing out that, when it all comes down to it, your heavenly Father is more important than anyone.

God is always there, waiting for you with outstretched arms whenever you need. Always ready to hold you close and listen to you, comfort you, love you.

There's really only one God. The one who knows you intimately and loves you completely.

» Get Real Maybe your own father has hurt you somehow, abandoned or disappointed you in some way. Human fathers are just that—human.

Let your heavenly Parent love you, and ask God to help you understand, accept, and love your earthly parents better.

» Dig In Read Matthew 23:1–7 to compare the way God acts with the way the Pharisees act. Can you imagine what the people thought about Jesus's words? How about what the Pharisees thought?

» Read On Jesus summarizes his teaching in Matthew 23:11–12, challenging believers to serve one another humbly. Then he goes on to really rip the selfish and self-righteous attitudes of the Pharisees in verses 13–36. Jesus pulls no punches. What does that tell you about what he's saying?

» Take Off Jesus called his Father "Abba," which is Aramaic for a title perhaps as tender as "Daddy." Meditate on that for a few moments. Think about the God who loves you the way a daddy loves his child, embracing you and comforting you.

DEVOTIONAL 42

Tuesday in Holy Week

Washing Your Dishes

Matthew 23:25–26
Woe to you, scribes and Pharisees, hypocrites! For you clean the outside of the cup and of the plate, but inside they are full of greed and self-indulgence. You blind Pharisee! First clean the inside of the cup, so that the outside also may become clean.

Looking Good on the Outside

On the outside, the Pharisees looked good. They dressed fancily. They kept clean. They were very careful to follow every dotted *i* and crossed *t* of the law about ceremonial cleanliness.

But God desires cleanness and holiness on the inside.

Jesus agreed that they did a good job cleaning the "outside of the cup and of the plate," but what good is a cup that is clean and shiny on the outside and full of stinky sludge on the inside? The Pharisees may have looked marvelous, but they were full of greed and selfishness on the inside, where it counts, where it can really make a mess.

Jesus says, first scrub out the inside of the cup with God's forgiveness, cleansing it through prayer, shining it with authenticity. That's how you make the cup of your life truly clean.

» Get Real How's your cup looking these days? What's it full of? What's it stained with? What's that crust of mold on the inside? Sure, you may look good externally, but is there anything internally you need to let God clean up?

» Dig In Where does today's passage fit in the flow of Matthew 23? What is Jesus doing with the Pharisees? Can you imagine how they must have reacted to his biting words?

» Read On Jesus is ripping the Pharisees, but his mood changes dramatically in verses 37–39. Who's he talking to there? What emotions do you sense? What ultimately happened when Jesus returned to Jerusalem on Palm Sunday?

» Take Off Jesus desires more than anything to help you dissolve that emotional sludge in your cup—to wash it away and fill your cup with his new wine of peace, forgiveness, and grace. Will you let him? He's listening.

⚜

Wednesday in Holy Week

Missing Out on Jesus's Love

Luke 13:34–35

Jerusalem, Jerusalem, the city that kills the prophets and stones those who are sent to it! How often have I desired to gather your children together as a hen gathers her brood under her wings, and you were not willing! See, your house is left to you. And I tell you, you will not see me until the time comes when you say, "Blessed is the one who comes in the name of the Lord."

The Heartbroken Messiah

In this encounter with Jerusalem before his Palm Sunday entry, Jesus's heart is already breaking. His own people have stubbornly rejected him as their Messiah. God has given them the incredible privilege of relating directly with Jesus as he walks the earth. But time after time they refuse him and his message—and it will only get worse.

As Jesus taught among them, the religious leaders kept their eyes and ears shut to God's truth. And now they are plotting to kill God's own Son.

Still, Jesus mourns over them. Even in the midst of the rejection, he longs to embrace them, to gather them together, to brood over them like a mother hen with warm love and acceptance. But they are not willing.

Could Jesus possibly be saying the same thing to you? He wants more than anything to be your liberator, your teacher, the lover of your soul. Climb in under his wings, knowing that you are his eternally beloved child.

» Get Real Is there a wall between you and Jesus—something keeping you from going all in with him? A fear of what it might mean, of where he'll take you, of what other people will think?

» Dig In Read the verses before today's text, Luke 13:31–33. Jesus has been wrangling with the Pharisees, the Jewish religious leaders. How do you think that led to his outburst over Jerusalem? How much did his realization of what was going to happen to him in Jerusalem in the days ahead affect him?

» Read On Compare this encounter Jesus had with Jerusalem with the one you read on Palm Sunday, Luke 19:41–44. Do you sense a different emotional tone in Jesus's words? What does this tell you about what's going on with Jesus as he faces the days ahead?

» Take Off Jesus doesn't hold back his feelings about those he loves. He wants more than anything to love and protect his children. Spend some time letting him do that for you.

Think About It
Preparing for the Triduum: Are You Ready?

Read John 13:1–17, 31b–35; Exodus 12:1–4, 11–14; 1 Corinthians 11:23–26

The Apostle Paul's words in 1 Corinthians 11 are warmly familiar: "This is my body . . . Do this in remembrance of me. . . . This cup is the new covenant in my blood, do this as often as you drink it in remembrance of me."

Paul is referring to the account in Luke 22 of the upper room, where Jesus institutes the sacrament of Holy Communion. And every week in church many follow that example. Those words have become meaningful and intimate to us. "Do this," Jesus tells us, and remember me as you do.

But in the lesson from John's gospel, we don't read anything about communion. John goes on for quite some time recounting Jesus's actions and teachings in the upper room before his arrest and crucifixion, as he prepares his disciples for what's next. But John talks about an entirely different sacrament, one Jesus also tells us to do in order to follow his example.

I'm talking about washing feet.

It only happens once a year, on Maundy Thursday, at least in our circles. We don't do it every week like we do the Eucharist, and so for that reason alone it's a little strange to us—maybe more than a little. Then add to the unfamiliarity of it the fact of what it actually involves: We have to take our shoes off and have someone wash our feet, and then turn around and wash their feet—perhaps the feet of someone we don't

75

even know well. No wonder we feel a little weird about it. It's way out of our comfort zone.

Each year on Maundy Thursday I can't help but remember what may have been the very first time I experienced a foot-washing ceremony, as a college student. Having been raised in the Methodist church, I honestly don't ever remember ever washing feet before this—if we did, I've blanked it out of my memory.

I was involved in the college fellowship group at a nearby Methodist church. A dear young woman, deeply earnest and committed, led the group. Debra really cared about our crazy lives in college. She was truly an example of humble service and love.

During Holy Week that year we came to our college group meeting at the church to find that our room had been transformed. The fluorescent lights were off; the room was bathed in subtle candlelight. Tablecloths covered a few tables, and on each table were a loaf of bread and a chalice of wine. And at the front of the room stood a stool, a basin, a pitcher, and some towels.

What the heck?

Debra explained what had happened in that upper room and announced that we were going to follow Jesus's example and wash each other's feet, and then we were going to share the bread and wine. When we realized what was about to happen with our feet, being college students and all, we giggled in embarrassment. Cracked a few jokes. In our discomfort it was a little hard to take it seriously.

But she was deadly serious.

And then, as we stood in a line to walk solemnly to the front of the room to get our feet washed, someone accidentally nudged into one of those tables—and a chalice of wine spilled over, splashing its contents all over the beautiful tablecloth. Well, with that all our pent-up embarrassment and shame exploded in laughter. We totally destroyed the mood, and I still feel a sharp pang of regret about that.

Oh, we managed to get through the rest of the service, but I can't forget that embarrassment and shame, the discomfort of washing feet and having our feet washed.

But then, the disciples felt the same way. At least Peter did. Jesus gets up from the table, takes off his outer robe, ties a towel around himself, pours water into a basin, and begins to wash their feet and dry them off with the towel. This must have stunned them—and finally Simon Peter says, "Lord, are *you* going to wash *my* feet? No way! You will never wash my feet!" It's just too weird.

But Jesus tells him, "Unless I wash you, you have no share with me." Well, when he puts it that way, Peter does a sudden 180-degree turn: "Lord, not my feet only but also my hands and my head!" Wash all of me, Jesus.

Peter misses the point. Jesus explains, "Hey, you're already clean. You've bathed in the past few weeks, you don't need to wash. Except for the feet, you're entirely clean—although not everyone here is clean." Of course he's hinting about the betrayer, Judas.

See, foot washing was a very important everyday practice in those days. As people walked the dusty or muddy roads from place to place, their feet became caked with dust and muck. It was essential to wash that stuff off. I remember as a kid when we spent our family vacation at Sunken Meadow Beach on the James River in Virginia, we always kept a basin of water by the front door of the cabin we rented to rinse the sand off our feet before we came in. It's the same kind of thing here. Perhaps they washed their own dirty feet, or more likely a servant did it as they arrived somewhere.

But for Jesus their rabbi and master to do it? It's astonishing.

Jesus is setting an example. He's telling his followers you should wash others' feet. That means you should serve humbly, love meaningfully, fulfill needs, even basic needs, serve others in some much-needed ways. And his love overcame their shame; his love smothered their embarrassment.

Jesus is preparing his companions for what's next. "Little children," he says, "I am with you only a little longer. . . ." He's getting them ready, telling them what's about to happen, and he's doing it with a love that overcomes their fear, their shame, their weirdness.

It's much like what the Lord tells Moses in Exodus 12 as the Israelites prepare to escape Egypt: "Be ready—loins girded, sandals on feet, staff in hand." Eat your Passover meal hurriedly, get ready for what's next. And now before the festival of the Passover in Jerusalem, Jesus is preparing his followers—he's washing their feet so they'll be ready to follow his example.

It's time to prepare ourselves as well. As Jesus told Peter, we've bathed already—in baptismal waters. Now we just need to get our feet washed and prepare for the difficult days ahead.

What are we getting ready for?

> » First we're in the upper room for Maundy Thursday.

> » Then comes Good Friday—the day Jesus is put to death on the cross, the day the disciples experience unimaginable fear and grief to the point many of them run away, at least for a while.

> » Then follows Holy Saturday, a time of waiting, not sure at all about what comes next. And next the Vigil, waiting for the coming dawn.

> » And finally the exuberant, surprising celebration of resurrection on Sunday, Easter Day.

That's what this preparation is for. We get our feet washed so we can be ready, loins girded, sandals on feet, prepared for what's next. Because after the resurrection, we face new opportunities to minister, to follow Jesus's example of humble service, meaningful love, and needed ministry. Jesus wants us to let him wash our feet so we can be ready to love and serve.

So Jesus sets the example. And his love overcomes his disciples' shame and discomfort. Now let his love overcome your hesitancy, your discomfort, your embarrassment, your shame.

Getting your feet washed is an example of what we can turn around and do for others by serving them humbly in meaningful and needed ways, even outside our comfort zone. What might that look like in your life? In your church? With your family and friends, in your neighborhood? What might that involve in this community? Jesus prepares us. Are you ready for what's next?

Yes, washing someone else's feet is weird. Yes, getting our feet washed is embarrassing. But it's a way Jesus offers to us to prepare ourselves to follow his example for humble, loving service.

"I give you a new commandment, that you love one another. Just as I have loved you, you also should love one another. By this everyone will know that you are my disciples, if you have love for one another."

So, are you ready for what's next? Are you ready to love?

Maundy Thursday

The Bread and the Wine

Mark 14:22–24

While they were eating, he took a loaf of bread, and after blessing it he broke it, gave it to them, and said, "Take; this is my body." Then he took a cup, and after giving thanks he gave it to them, and all of them drank from it. He said to them, "This is my blood of the covenant, which is poured out for many."

The Bittersweet Banquet

Jesus joins his closest friends in an upstairs room for a final meal together. The fellowship is bittersweet. The events that loom ahead of him haunt their gathering.

As they observe the Passover meal, Jesus takes the bread, thanks God for it, breaks it, and gives it to his disciples. Perhaps his words startle them: "Take; this is my body." The Bread of Life, his body, is about to be broken for all. And whenever we eat the bread of the Eucharist, we remember his sacrifice on the cross the following day. By eating the bread, we bring Jesus and his mission into our life anew.

Then Jesus offers them the cup of wine, fully realizing what it represents: his own blood. Blood that marks the beginning of a new covenant—a new relationship between God and humanity. A promise of grace, mercy, freedom, acceptance. A promise that stands forever, signifying that we belong to God forever because we belong to God's Son.

Eat it. Drink it in. Experience it. Understand it. Accept it. And thank him for it.

» Get Real See yourself in the huddle of the upper room, reclining around the table, hearing Jesus invite you to partake. How do you feel? What do you sense? What are your fears, your questions, your emotions? Bring all this to the altar next time your church celebrates the Eucharist.

» Dig In Note what happened just before this in Mark 14:17–21. How does that add to your understanding of what Jesus himself was feeling when he broke the bread and shared the wine?

» Read On Read verse 25—what did Jesus mean by this? Do you think this has anything to do with what happened in Mark 15:23? How do you think they relate?

» Take Off Jesus gave his all for us. And he wants us to realize that—and remember it. Not just when your church celebrates the Eucharist, but daily, moment by moment. Spend some time in thankful prayer for what Jesus has accomplished on your behalf.

DEVOTIONAL 45

Good Friday

The Pain of Abandonment

Matthew 27:45–46, 50

From noon on, darkness came over the whole land until three in the afternoon. And about three o'clock Jesus cried with a loud voice, "Eli, Eli, lema sabachthani?" that is, "My God, my God, why have you forsaken me?". . . . Then Jesus cried again with a loud voice and breathed his last.

Incomprehensible Agony

Naked. Bleeding. Bruised. Crushed. Broken. Hanging by his skin and bones on a rough wooden cross. Darkness has fallen over the land. A chilling darkness of the soul. Silence reigns.

A few people huddle around him, either to curse him or to mourn for him. And with a loud voice, he cries out to his Father. His Daddy has seemingly forsaken him. Abandoned him. Left him completely out in the cold. Physically, emotionally, spiritually. Why? *Why?*

The pain of the spikes through his wrists and ankles is nothing compared to the pain of his broken heart.

It was your pain he carried that day. Your cry on his lips. He knows how you feel. And at this very moment, he's praying for you. Let him carry your pain of abandonment and fear right now. After all, he has already experienced it for you. And for all.

» Get Real Can you see yourself there, huddled before the cross, horrified by Jesus's plight? Your Master writhing in agony, barely able to breathe? Why did he do it?

» Dig In Why do you think Jesus uttered the words of Psalm 22? What is that psalm about? Whose experience is captured in that psalm? How do those verses foreshadow the agony Christ experienced on the cross?

» Read On Carefully read the whole account of the crucifixion slowly and carefully in Matthew 27:32–56. What parts of it stand out for you? What parts hurt you, surprise you, or confuse you?

» Take Off We can never really understand what Jesus experienced on the cross. But, thank God, we don't have to. Let your thoughts about that watershed event in human history—and in your own relationship with God—prompt you to a time of prayer and praise.

DEVOTIONAL 46

Holy Saturday

A Soul Swallowed Up in Sorrow

Mark 14:32–34

They went to a place called Gethsemane; and he said to his disciples, "Sit here while I pray." He took with him Peter and James and John, and began to be distressed and agitated. And he said to them, "I am deeply grieved, even to death; remain here, and keep awake."

Companionship in Dark Times

Can you imagine how Jesus's companions feel on Holy Saturday? The day after they witnessed his grueling death on the cross? A day they are likely hiding in fear and grief? Just like you have felt at times, no doubt.

This passage makes one thing totally clear: Jesus understands how you feel when you are at your lowest. Because he's been there too. On the night before his crucifixion he was so swallowed up in sorrow in the Garden of Gethsemane that it nearly killed him.

At that dark time, Jesus asked his friends to stay with him. To just be with him. To support him with their presence. He needed human companionship in his toughest, loneliest hour. And he asked for it directly. They must have felt much the same way on that Holy Saturday.

When we need the supportive touch of someone we trust, when we just need to be heard and accepted where we are, those times can be the hardest to ask for what we need. When you find yourself in that place, follow Jesus's example. Ask for what you need.

And if you have trouble finding someone to be there with you, remember that Jesus always is.

» Get Real We'll never understand what the disciples felt on Holy Saturday, or what Jesus was going through on that Maundy Thursday night, waiting to be hung on a tree. But know that when you get overwhelmed, horrified, or wiped out, he knows. And he is with you in it.

» Dig In Jesus's remaining disciples were with him in the Garden, but only Peter, James, and John were close by him. Why do you think that was? What did he want them to do for him?

» Read On Jesus's disciples were so human. Just like us. Read Mark 14:37–42 and see how well they offered Jesus their support. If someone asked for your help and support in a tough time, you'd do better than that, right?

» Take Off In the Garden, Jesus asked the Father to spare him of this agony, to take away the mammoth responsibility he faced (v. 36). But he ultimately gave himself to his Father's will, knowing full well what that meant. What does it mean to you? Talk to God about it.

Think About It
Easter Vigil: "This Is the Night"

Read Genesis 1:1–2, 4a; Exodus 14:10–31, 15:20–21; Isaiah 55:1–11; Ezekiel 37:1–14; Zephaniah 3:14–20; Romans 6:3–11; Luke 24:1–12

Have you ever found yourself in complete, total darkness? The kind where you can't see your hand in front of your face? It can be a terrifying place.

My parents once told me about a particular Saturday when I was about four years old. They were sitting in the kitchen and heard a stifled cry. They couldn't tell where it was coming from. And they panicked.

"It sounds like Peter! Where is he? What's wrong?" They searched the bedrooms upstairs, the closets, the pantry—nothing. They couldn't find me. Finally, Dad tracked the cries to a tiny storage compartment outside the basement, under the back steps. It had a tight door. Apparently it was so dark in this little space where I'd crawled for whatever reason that I was unable to move. I was powerless. The door was jammed and I was stuck in this small space in total darkness.

Dad yanked the door open and pulled me out. The strange thing is, I have no recollection of this. I think my mind blanked out the memory of being stuck in a place of utter darkness and powerlessness.

Have you ever been in a place like that? Maybe you haven't been stuck in a small storage compartment, but sometimes it sure can feel like it. It is the darkness of the loss of someone dear to us, whose absence we fear we'll never be able to deal with. The darkness of a terrifying diagnosis.

The darkness of not knowing where a child of ours is. The darkness of a shattering reality that we had no idea was coming our way.

The Easter Vigil service begins in darkness. It is the darkness of the closed-up tomb where Jesus's body lay on Holy Saturday. The stone has been rolled in front of it. No light enters. It is utterly dark. Jesus's torn and beaten body is already beginning to stink—the women are planning to bring spices in the morning to help preserve his corpse. But now it is Saturday, in the dark, airless, deathly still tomb. It is not a pleasant place to be.

Unlike the hosannas of Palm Sunday and the glory of the Easter dawn that we yearn for, this day in Holy Week can relate deeply to our everyday lives—those dark moments when we get bad news about our health or finances, a broken relationship, or the loss of a loved one. We wonder what in the world can possibly happen next—and then it does. And we must live in a time and space of darkness, trying to trust in the God of resurrections.

This is the place where each of us may find ourselves time and again. Yes, there are moments when we experience the dark, gut-wrenching pain of Good Friday, and there are moments when we know the jubilation of Easter. But Holy Saturday is the time in between death and resurrection, a valley of unknowing—just as it was for Jesus's disciples.

"In the beginning, when God created the heavens and the earth, the earth was a formless void and darkness covered the face of the deep. . . " (Gen. 1:1–2a).

In the beginning, all was a dark void. And in the tomb where Jesus lay we find the same reality—a dark void. How many times will we find ourselves in that place? A place where any ray of hope is extinguished in the vacuum of fear, of not knowing, of total emptiness?

Somehow, through the grace of God, we must be patient in that place. We must wait for the wind of the Spirit, the "wind from God [that sweeps] over the face of the waters" in Genesis 1, to fan the dim embers of our faith.

"Then God said, 'Let there be light,' and there was light. . . ." Oh—thank you, God. "God called the light Day and the darkness he called Night. And there was evening and there was morning, the first day" (Gen. 1:3, 5).

You see, both darkness and light are part of the first day. Darkness and light are halves of every day ever since that first day. Darkness and light are essential parts of our lives. And when we find ourselves in that dark, tight, stinky, lonely place, we must remind ourselves of this truth. There will always, ultimately, be light in the midst of the darkness.

In Exodus 14, as God leads Moses and the Israelites out of Egypt at night, the Israelites cry out to God in fear and uncertainty as they see the massive army of Pharaoh in pursuit behind them, while in front of them is the sea; they are trapped in the darkness of fear and faithlessness.

"It would have been better for us to serve the Egyptians than to die in the wilderness," they cry out. But Moses tells them, "Do not be afraid, stand firm, and see the deliverance that the Lord will accomplish for you today. . . . The Lord will fight for you, and *you have only to keep still.*"

It's so hard to keep still in the fearful dark, isn't it? So hard to wait and trust that the wind of God's Spirit will, eventually, finally, blow on the dim embers of our cooling faith.

And notice verses 19 and 20: "The angel of God who was going before the Israelite army moved and went *behind* them; and the pillar of cloud moved from in front of them and took its place *behind* them." Why? "It came *between* the army of Egypt and the army of Israel. And so the cloud was there with the darkness, and it lit up the night."

So the divine presence, the angel of God, glowing within the cloud in the darkness, blocks the oncoming threat of the Egyptian army. See, there will always be light in the midst of darkness. God *will* show up at night. We have only to keep still. And wait. That's what the Easter Vigil is all about: waiting.

Darkness is part of every day. But there will be light. What would our lives with God look like if we trusted this rhythm of darkness and light instead of fighting it?

The *Exsultet,* traditionally chanted at the Easter Vigil, so beautifully proclaims this rhythm of dark and light, of night and dawn, of death and resurrection:

> *This is the night* . . . when you brought our [ancestors], the children of Israel, out of bondage in Egypt. . . .

> *This is the night* . . . when all who believe in Christ are delivered from the gloom of sin, and are restored to grace and holiness of life. . . .

> *This is the night* . . . when Christ broke the bonds of death and hell, and rose victorious from the grave. . . .

> How holy is this night, when wickedness is put to flight, and sin is washed away. It restores innocence to the fallen, and joy to those who mourn. . . .

> How blessed is this night, when earth and heaven are joined and we are reconciled to God.[4]

Even in the darkness of our lives—darkness that comes and goes like the night—we are reconciled to God.

We may find ourselves in darkness right now, but just wait. Wait for the dawn of hope and resurrection.

It's coming.

---

4   The Episcopal Church, *The Book of Common Prayer and Administration of the Sacraments and Other Rites and Ceremonies of the Church: Together with the Psalter or Psalms of David According to the Use of the Episcopal Church* (New York: Church Publishing, Inc., 1979), 286–87. Emphasis added.

DEVOTIONAL 47

Easter Day

Seeing the Risen Jesus

Matthew 28:5–10

The angel said to the women, "Do not be afraid; I know that you are looking for Jesus who was crucified. He is not here; for he has been raised, as he said. Come, see the place where he lay. Then go quickly and tell his disciples, 'He has been raised from the dead, and indeed he is going ahead of you to Galilee; there you will see him.' This is my message for you." So they left the tomb quickly with fear and great joy, and ran to tell his disciples. Suddenly Jesus met them and said, "Greetings!" And they came to him, took hold of his feet, and worshiped him. Then Jesus said to them, "Do not be afraid; go and tell my brothers to go to Galilee; there they will see me."

A Senses-Shattering Surprise

The women who go to his tomb to care for Jesus's hurriedly buried body experience something no human could have been prepared for—an angel, an empty tomb, a word of comfort: "Do not be afraid."

And that's not all. On their way back to tell the others the good news, reckless with joy and amazement, they meet Jesus himself. "Greetings!" he says to them. The brightest morning ever follows the darkest possible night.

The women fall to the ground in worship, grabbing hold of his feet. And he too tells them, "Do not be afraid."

Jesus has escaped death. He lives again. Go and tell—that's all the women can do. Everything else—all the pains and fears and frustrations of their lives—fade away. All that is left is a risen Savior.

And that is enough.

» Get Real Jesus is risen today. And he still encourages you not to be afraid, but to go and tell. How will you respond to that? How does your life look and feel when you set it into the context of the resurrection of your Lord?

» Dig In Why do you think the angel told the women not to be afraid? Why did Jesus? The angel and Jesus both gave them instructions and they promptly obeyed. Why do you think they so carefully instructed the women to go tell the disciples?

» Read On Read the setup to this passage, Matthew 28:1–4, to catch an exciting glimpse of what happened at the resurrection. Can you imagine being there, seeing this? Try.

» Take Off Reading Matthew 28 can send you soaring spiritually. This is the Jesus who lives today, the Jesus who tells *you* not to be afraid. Who encourages you to go and tell. Who is with you always. Who loves it when you talk with him.

Think About It
Now What?
Week after Easter and Beyond

Read Luke 24:36b–48

Just after Easter a few years ago, I came across an online news article reporting on an Anglican priest who said he was "gobsmacked" by a post-Easter experience. I love that word "gobsmacked," because it's more fun to say it than to say "utterly astonished" or "astounded."

Well, what could an Anglican priest in Cambridgeshire, England, possibly be gobsmacked about regarding Easter? It had to be some incredible spiritual experience, right?

I clicked on the link. The headline read, "'Gobsmacked' reverend refused entry to bar for wearing sandals because of health and safety." The story reported that a local vicar celebrating the end of Lent was refused service at a local bar because he was wearing open sandals and they feared that broken glass on the floor would harm his feet. The priest claimed he was "gobsmacked" by being ejected, wearing his collar and everything, but soon thereafter was able to enjoy his celebration at another bar.[5]

Well! Gobsmacked for being refused service at a bar. Apparently, the reverend posted his story on his social media accounts and it became quite the brouhaha.

---

5 "'Gobsmacked' reverend who hails from March refused entry to bar for wearing sandals because of health and safety," *Wisbech Standard*, April 8, 2015, http://www.wisbechstandard. co.uk/news/gobsmacked_reverend_who_hails_from_march_refused_entry_to_bar_ for_wearing_sandals_because_of_health_and_safety_1_4025959.

Luke offers us another, more valuable story about gobsmacked people just after Easter. And these people were truly gobsmacked, astounded, astonished. They were the disciples in the upper room.

They have gathered there in their excitement, confusion, joy, and fear, sharing various stories about sightings of the risen Jesus, wondering what it all meant. And suddenly, Jesus himself is standing in their midst.

Can you imagine it? Jesus says, "Peace be with you," and certainly, peace was the last thing they were feeling in that moment. In fact, Luke says they are startled, terrified—they thought they were seeing a ghost. In other words, they are gobsmacked.

Jesus questions them: "Why are you frightened? Why do doubts arise in your hearts?" They must have been standing around him with mouths open, the whites of their eyes showing in astonishment, doubting their very sanity. "Look at my hands and my feet; see that it is I myself." They could still see the brutal scars of crucifixion on his resurrected body.

Then Jesus goes beyond inviting them to look and see. He says, "Touch me and see."

He was touchable, truly flesh and blood, not a ghost. Luke doesn't record whether any of the disciples actually did touch him at his invitation, but he does say this: "While in their joy they were disbelieving and still wondering." Their emotions were in a turmoil of shock, joy, doubt, hope, astonishment. The original Greek word for this is *gobsmacked*.[6]

The disciples stand there in shock looking at their beloved rabbi, no doubt frozen in place, and then out of the blue Jesus asks, "Have you anything here to eat?" Perhaps he wants to further prove to his friends that he is truly living flesh and blood, not a spirit. So they give him some fish sticks and he eats them in their presence.

---

6 I'm kidding.

Then he leads a Bible study with them: "He opened their minds to understand the scriptures," everything that Moses, the prophets, and the psalms said about him. Jesus must have loved doing that, because just before this encounter he had done the same thing with the couple on the road to Emmaus.

Perhaps to these gobsmacked disciples, finally it all makes sense—why Jesus had to suffer and die and rise from the dead. It was all there all the time in the words of their Scripture. And Jesus helps them see it.

Then Jesus tells them what's next: "Repentance and forgiveness of sins is to be proclaimed in his name to all nations, beginning from Jerusalem." Why? Because "You are witnesses to these things."

You are witnesses to these things. And these doubting, fearful, shocked, gobsmacked disciples would soon turn the world upside down for Jesus Christ.

Well, here's where I experience some frustration. Because I didn't get to look and see Jesus. I didn't get to look at his brutalized hands and feet. I didn't get to touch him and see. I didn't get to watch him eat those broiled fish sticks. I didn't get my mind opened by Jesus so that I could understand all the scriptures. Frankly, I'm a little jealous of these disciples. I hear Jesus's challenge to be a witness to these things, and I counter, yes, but, I didn't witness them. I want to be gobsmacked, like the disciples were. Then I'm sure I can be a good witness.

But wait, I tell myself, Luke's story is still unfolding. Some days from now, these disciples will witness their risen Lord ascending into heaven. And not long after that, they will experience the coming of the Holy Spirit at Pentecost, giving them power to fulfill their calling as witnesses to these things. And that same Holy Spirit dwells within me, and within you, giving us the power to be witnesses, too.

Ah! The Spirit of the risen Christ, the Spirit of the living God, the Holy Spirit dwells within us so that we, like the disciples, may be his witnesses. And look what they accomplished in the power of the Spirit.

So what might we do? Will we tell a friend about the new life we've found by worshiping and serving Jesus? Will we help teach in our church's Sunday school, or volunteer to help lead a Bible study? Will we participate in a Habitat for Humanity home build or volunteer at a soup kitchen? Will we provide needed resources for worthy ministries in our communities?

In all of these ways and many more, we are bearing witness to the life, death, and resurrection of Jesus. We are in a way proclaiming repentance and the forgiveness of sins. We are sharing new life in Jesus to the world around us.

And when we do, we better prepare ourselves to be gobsmacked by Jesus.

DEVOTIONAL 48

Monday in Easter Week

A World of Hurt

Matthew 25:34–36

Then the king will say to those at his right hand, "Come, you that are blessed by my Father, inherit the kingdom prepared for you from the foundation of the world; for I was hungry and you gave me food, I was thirsty and you gave me something to drink, I was a stranger and you welcomed me, I was naked and you gave me clothing, I was sick and you took care of me, I was in prison and you visited me."

Turning Away from Jesus

It's easy to turn away when you see a street person holding a weathered cardboard sign asking for food money. When a stranger looks lost, needy, hurting, we avoid eye contact. And the sick, the prisoners—someone else can take care of them.

But wait. Jesus is saying *he* is the hungry, the thirsty, the stranger, the naked, the sick, the prisoner. And when we reach out to those in desperate need, we are in reality reaching out to him.

There are many hurting people around you. What can you do? How can you minister for Jesus—and *to* Jesus? How can your church reach out to people in need in your community—at a soup kitchen, a nursing home, an after-school program for underprivileged kids, a family shelter? This is how Easter people live. Talk about it with others at your church.

And as you do, remember Jesus's words: "Truly I tell you, just as you did it to one of the least of these who are members of my family, you did it to me" (Matt. 25:40).

» Get Real What can one person do? You'd be amazed. Think about how you feel when someone goes out of their way to help you or make you feel better. Now imagine the blessing you'll receive being the one who gets to share God's love.

» Dig In What's the context of this story Jesus tells? Read Matthew 25:31–33. How do the righteous people respond to the king here? Why?

» Read On Keep reading through to the end of Matthew 25. Note the different responses of the righteous and the unrighteous. So what happens if you ignore a God-given opportunity to minister in Jesus's name? And how valid is the excuse, "I didn't know"?

» Take Off Look at the world with Jesus's eyes and you'll likely see Jesus looking back at you. Are you willing to try? To take that risky step of obedience? Prepare yourself in prayer right now.

DEVOTIONAL 49

Tuesday in Easter Week

Total Authority

Matthew 28:16–18

Now the eleven disciples went to Galilee, to the mountain to which Jesus had directed them. When they saw him, they worshiped him; but some doubted. And Jesus came and said to them, "All authority in heaven and on earth has been given to me."

The Person in Charge

Just before he left earth in his resurrection body, Jesus met with his closest friends. They'd been spending time with him during the astonishing days after his death and resurrection, witnessing strange sights and seeing their rabbi in a new light. And now he is giving them his final words.

In doing so, he reveals that his words have the full force and authority of the God of the universe behind them. Because God the holy Parent has given him all authority over heaven and earth.

Sure, there are times in your life when it seems like no one is in control—even Jesus. Times of loneliness, chaos, weakness, pain. But those are the very times to turn to the one who is in authority over you and your world. Because he has the power to act in the will of God.

» Get Real Join the huddle of the disciples as they listen to Jesus speak. See him in his radiant resurrection body. Experience the pure, clean joy of knowing this person personally, as a close friend. Because you do.

» Dig In Take a closer look at verse 17. They saw Jesus and worshiped him, "but some doubted." Why do you think that was? What did Jesus do in response?

» Read On Jesus declares that he possesses all authority. Then, on the basis of that reality, he gives his disciples their marching orders in verses 19–20. What are those orders? What should we remember when we follow them ourselves?

» Take Off You serve a God who knows what's happening, who knows you inside and out, who loves you, who wants to be present with you, guiding and challenging you. Can you hear God speak to you today? What will you say in response?

⚜

DEVOTIONAL 50

Wednesday in Easter Week

Go!

Mark 16:15–16

And he said to them, "Go into all the world and proclaim the good news to the whole creation. The one who believes and is baptized will be saved; but the one who does not believe will be condemned."

A Heart as Big as the World

The resurrected Jesus has his eyes set on the whole world. And that's where he encourages his followers to go.

"All the world . . . the whole creation." That means everywhere and everyone. See, there are no limits to the good news. No one can be excluded from its endless circle of grace.

It's easy to get boxed up in our own culture, our own ethnic group or clique, our own set ways and pet beliefs. And as we do, our "world" gets smaller and smaller. Our eyes become more and more nearsighted. That's not Jesus's way. His eyes scan the far horizons seeking those who need God's love.

We can go. We can pray. But what we shouldn't do is keep our focus too tight.

All the world. The whole creation. God's heart is that big. Is yours?

» Get Real How far have you been looking lately? Do you find yourself so caught up in your own life that you can't see past your nose? There's a whole world out there that needs to meet Jesus. What can you do about it?

» Dig In Notice Jesus isn't offering a suggestion; he's issuing an imperative: "Go." What happens with those we go to is between them and God. Our responsibility is just to love them enough to go to them. Think about that as you read verse 16 again.

» Read On So what happened next? How did the disciples respond? Read Mark 16:19–20 and find out.

» Take Off What will it take to get you to accept Jesus's challenge? Is it fear that holds you back? Too busy with your own stuff? Not sure how to go about it? Talk to Jesus about all that. And then talk with your friends too.

DEVOTIONAL 51

Thursday in Easter Week

The Eternal Companion

Matthew 28:20b
And remember, I am with you always, to the end of the age.

Famous Last Words
Jesus leaves his disciples with a helpful reminder: He is always with us. Right where we are. In our hearts and lives. In our pain and problems. In our fears and frustrations. In our loneliness and laziness.

It's a reality that's easy to forget, because we get so distracted by our life circumstances that we fail to remember there's someone right here with us who knows us, knows everything about us. One who can use our circumstances for our own good.

No matter what we do. No matter what happens to us. He will always, always be with us. Over us. Under us. Before us. Behind us. Beside us. Inside us.

Jesus will never leave us or turn his back on us. We are his beloved siblings. He yearns to see us grow stronger in his love and in our spirit. And if you'll let him, he will be working with you to fulfill his calling for your life, even to the end of the age.

» Get Real How constantly do you keep this relationship with Jesus in your conscious mind? How often do you feel you're totally on your own in this world? How well will you remember this reality from now on?

» Dig In Jesus tells us to "remember." He must've known the disciples would struggle with this, since they were used to seeing him day by day in the flesh. We're in a better position than even they were. Because Jesus is right inside us.

» Read On Jesus reminded Paul of the same truth in Acts 18:9–11. What does this passage tell you about what Jesus wants to do with and for us?

» Take Off Let it sink in: Jesus is with you always. Right now. And forever. Have you sensed his presence today? Pray as though he's sitting right here with you, because it's true.

DEVOTIONAL 52

Friday in Easter Week

The Most Important Commandment

Matthew 22:35–40

And one of them, a lawyer, asked him a question to test him. "Teacher, which commandment in the law is the greatest?" He said to him, "'You shall love the Lord your God with all your heart, and with all your soul, and with all your mind.' This is the greatest and first commandment. And a second is like it: 'You shall love your neighbor as yourself.' On these two commandments hang all the law and the prophets."

Loving God with All You Have

Put to the test once again by the religious elite, Jesus boiled down all their dos and don'ts by quoting a verse from Deuteronomy 6. It's the first thing God's children should do: Love God.

Love God with your *whole heart*. With all the affection and attention and emotion God deserves—which is all of it.

Love God with your *whole soul*. With every fiber of who you are—your personality, your gifts, your whole way of living.

Love God with your *whole mind*. Intelligently, questioningly, probingly, thoughtfully.

Loving God involves your whole being. Every cell of your existence should be aimed toward loving the one who made you, keeps you going, provides for you, and loves you more than you could ever, ever love in return.

And then, do something that arises naturally from your relationship with God: Love your neighbor as yourself. Pursue these goals and you will carry the lively, loving spirit of Easter with you all year long—and for the rest of your life.

» Get Real So how's your relationship with God? How much of yourself—your heart, mind, and soul—are you giving God? Or are you, like the Pharisees, too caught up in all the intricate dos and don'ts you think God wants you to follow in order to be accepted?

» Dig In Read verse 34 and you'll see the Pharisees and Sadducees are playing "tag team wrestling" with Jesus. They may not have gotten along together very well, but they were united in their opposition to Jesus. Why?

» Read On Keep reading in Matthew 22:41–46 and listen to the rest of the verbal jousting between Jesus and the Pharisees. Jesus turns the tables, asking them a question to trip them up a bit. How did the Pharisees answer him? What happened after that?

» Take Off Take some time to think back through your journey of listening to Jesus and getting to know him again through this holy season. Center in on the love you have for God right now. Feel it, know it, live it. And shine with God's love for all your neighbors. Today and forever.

Think About It
Looking Back, Moving Forward

Okay, here we are. The last page. We could have left it blank. You could flip past it quickly, slap the book closed, and move on with your life.

But no. This moment is too important to pass by.

Because this is an opportunity for you to do something about everything you've read and prayed about and meditated on and written down in a journal.

Take just a moment and think about it all. Then try to put your thoughts into some words as you pray about these questions:

> » *What have I learned about Jesus?*
>
> » *What have I learned about myself?*
>
> » *What have I learned about my life purpose, my mission?*
>
> » *What changes have I seen in my life through these past 52 days?*
>
> » *What changes do I want to see happen that haven't yet?*

Here's a prayer that I hope will launch you into an ongoing conversation with Jesus:

> Jesus, you are holy, you are awe-inspiring, you are real. More real to me than you've ever been. Because I've gotten to see you up close, in action. I've listened to your words afresh. I've come to sense your presence with me in deeper, stronger ways. I've heard your call on my life—to live a righteous, empowered, beloved, sacrificial life, just as you did. And I know you will provide everything I need to do that. I give

myself to you and your call. Totally. Wholeheartedly. I open the door of my future to you, to guide me, to be who I need to be. All driven and filled and empowered by the Holy Spirit whom you've given to dwell within me. It's you and me now, Jesus, forever and ever. Thank you. Amen.

> **"Those who find their life will lose it, and those who lose their life for my sake will find it."**
>
> **—Matthew 10:39**

In the life of faith, paradoxes abound. This is one of them.

Jesus says that in discovering genuine life, life with him, you will lose life, life as you now know it.

The life you have been living may have been self-focused, weak, empty, and powerless—just a shadow of what is possible, of what in fact is promised.

Losing that life—submitting it in open-handed faith to God—is the doorway to finding a far better life:

» A life that's not without its struggles and pain, but one that offers comfort, encouragement, and growth in the midst of it all.

» A life that over time becomes less greedy and more generous, because the internal resources out of which you can give have increased exponentially.

» A life that becomes richer and more fulfilling day by day, because the hassles of life don't have such a stranglehold over you anymore, and you can see the beauty and purpose of it all instead.

Today, this kind of life is within your grasp. But first you have to let go of your own way of life. And choose God's.

Scripture Index

About the Author

The Rev. Peter Marsden Wallace is the author of ten books, including *The Passionate Jesus: What We Can Learn from Jesus about Love, Fear, Grief, Joy and Living Authentically*; *Connected: You and God in the Psalms*; *Living Loved: Knowing Jesus as the Lover of Your Soul*; and *Out of the Quiet: Responding to God's Whispered Invitations.* He has contributed to numerous books, study Bibles, devotional guides, magazines, teaching curricula, video series, and other resources. He blogs at Huffpost.com and Day1.org. Peter is executive producer and host of the national ecumenical "Day1" radio and internet ministry (Day1.org) and president of the Alliance for Christian Media, based in Atlanta, Georgia. The weekly Day1 radio program, the voice of the historic mainline Protestant churches, is distributed to more than 220 radio stations across America and overseas.

Peter earned a bachelor's degree in journalism/advertising from Marshall University and a master of theology degree from Dallas Theological Seminary, Texas. He completed Anglican studies courses at Candler School of Theology at Emory University. He has been a confirmed member of the Episcopal Church since 1991, and was ordained as an Episcopal priest in 2014 and serves in the Diocese of Atlanta. He lives in Atlanta with his spouse, Daniel Le.